Safer Faiths, Safer Followers

Safer Faiths, Safer Followers

Understanding and Countering Spiritual Abuse in Faith Communities

Tom Wilson

CANTERBURY
PRESS

© Tom Wilson 2025

First published in 2025 by the Canterbury Press Norwich

Editorial office
3rd Floor, Invicta House
110 Golden Lane,
London EC1Y 0TG, UK
www.canterburypress.co.uk

Canterbury Press is an imprint of Hymns Ancient & Modern Ltd
(a registered charity)

Hymns Ancient & Modern® is a registered trademark of
Hymns Ancient & Modern Ltd
13A Hellesdon Park Road, Norwich,
Norfolk NR6 5DR, UK

All rights reserved. No part of this publication may be reproduced,
stored in a retrieval system, or transmitted,
in any form or by any means, electronic, mechanical,
photocopying or otherwise, without the prior permission of
the publisher, Canterbury Press.

No part of this book may be used or reproduced in any manner for the
purpose of training artificial intelligence technologies or systems.

The Author has asserted his right under the Copyright, Designs and
Patents Act 1988 to be identified as the Author of this Work

British Library Cataloguing in Publication data

A catalogue record for this book is available
from the British Library

Scripture quotations are from New Revised Standard Version Bible:
Anglicized Edition, copyright © 1989, 1995 National Council of the
Churches of Christ in the United States of America. Used by permission.
All rights reserved worldwide.

ISBN: 978-1-78622-704-1

EU GPSR Authorised Representative
LOGOS EUROPE, 9 rue Nicolas Poussin, 17000, LA ROCHELLE, France
E-mail: Contact@logoseurope.eu

Typeset by Regent Typesetting

Contents

Introduction: Trust Matters   1

Part I: Understanding   7

1   What Are We Talking About?   9

Part II: Conversations   21

2   Conversations about Spiritual Abuse   23
3   Responses of Different Religions   38
4   The Power of Choice and Learning   51

Part III: Lessons   65

5   Spiritual Abuse in the Church of England   67
6   Faith, Power and Abuse: A Christian Reflection   100

Part IV: Next Steps   123

7   Working with the Authorities   125
8   Raising Awareness in Your Community   135
9   Sample Sermons for Safeguarding Sunday   154

Conclusion: The Way Forward   168

Bibliography   169

Introduction: Trust Matters

> The walk up the path to the shed was agonizing. We always held hands. It was a two-minute walk from the house. Sometimes we would walk in silence. Sometimes I would ask how many I would get this time. Trips to the shed were never quick. Quick beatings happened in the house, in his study or the upstairs bathroom. The shed was about the experience. The experience often began days before. My dad was often away all week and returned at the weekends. Mum would write my wrong-doings in 'the book' in the kitchen ready for my dad to read on his return. I had days of waiting. Days of anticipating my next visit to the shed. (P. J. Smyth recalls the impact of the abuse he suffered at his father's hands; Makin, 2024, p. 23)

This quote, taken from the Makin Review into the abuse perpetrated by John Smyth, illustrates the devastating impact of all forms of abuse. The testimony of those individuals who have experienced spiritual abuse is that spiritual abuse destroys the ability of individuals and groups to trust. And where there is no trust, there is no certainty, and life cannot flourish. As Brené Brown observes:

> Betrayal is so painful because, at its core, it is a violation of trust. It happens in relationships in which trust is expected and assumed, so when it is violated, we're often shocked, and we can struggle to believe what's happening. It can feel as if the ground beneath us has given way. (Brown, 2021, p. 194)

Many religious leaders, institutions and organizations have betrayed people of faith. The damage is incalculable. Yet something must be done. My purpose in writing this short book is to provide opportunities for understanding and countering the reality of spiritual abuse: both to recognize the nature of the problem and to come up with ways of responding that restore trust, rebuild shattered lives and encourage hope. I have been ordained in the Church of England for more than 15 years and have extensive experience of interreligious and community work. I am writing, in many senses, from a place of privilege and power, with a desire to use that privilege and power for the good of the marginalized, the poor, the oppressed and the downtrodden. But I am not a legal expert; nor am I a psychotherapist. What follows should not be construed as legal advice or as a substitute for therapy.

All forms of abuse are destructive; spiritual abuse especially so. During my research, I spoke with a Christian who works in safeguarding. He said:

> The impact of abuse in a spiritual setting has the capacity to go even deeper than any other type of abuse ... If we have ascribed spiritual leadership to an individual, that seems to go hand in hand with a fairly deep level of trust. So, if the person in that spiritual place then takes advantage of that trust and is abusive ... it seems to also hit something even deeper around our level of trust. And that becomes a hugely destabilizing factor in somebody's sense of certainty and solidity about life.

My work in responding to issues raised by spiritual abuse began in 2017, when I was asked to research safeguarding practices in UK-based Buddhist and Hindu communities. This work led to an event in 2019: a small workshop held at the St Philip's Centre, Leicester, that brought together people of different religions to talk about spiritual abuse. With the help of Buddhist, Christian, Hindu, Jewish, Muslim and Sikh colleagues, I have now written case studies and scenarios to help people think about the reality of spiritual abuse, as well as conducting ethnographic research that explores people's understanding and experience of spiritual abuse.

The research on which this book is based took place in two phases. The first of these was as a dissertation for a Master's

INTRODUCTION: TRUST MATTERS

in Public Administration at the University of Birmingham. This research was carried out primarily in 2023. The second phase occurred after the dissertation had been submitted, in spring 2024.

Where I am coming from

Before explaining more about my research, I will tell you a bit about myself, to help you understand my perspective. Although I personally have never experienced spiritual abuse, since 2017 I have had numerous conversations with individuals who have experienced it. I am the director of the St Philip's Centre, which is a small charity. It is an interfaith training and resourcing organization. The charity has a Christian foundation and works closely with Christians of different denominations and perspectives. We also draw alongside people of all religious perspectives and none, including humanists and the Leicester Secular Society. We help congregations and those training for authorized Christian ministry, as well as schools, colleges, universities and private companies; we also collaborate with the police, fire and rescue services, the NHS, and city and county councils. We run community-based projects, including those that support religious organizations to improve their safeguarding policies and procedures.

My academic training and experience are as a linguist and an ethnographer, as well as an analyst of sacred texts. These are the three prongs of my academic and day-to-day approach to any problem. In the case of spiritual abuse, they form a useful toolkit.

First, my training as a linguist is relevant because words matter: words can hurt; words can destroy. What we say (and what we do not say) has an impact on us and those around us. Words can wound. A flippant comment might leave a deep and lasting scar. The use of language within the context of spiritual abuse is important. Listening to what is said helps us to pay attention to power.

Second, I conducted my PhD research as an ethnographer. The focus of that research was on Muslim experiences in a Church of England primary school. The specifics do not matter so much as the generic skills that are integral to ethnography. You learn to watch, to observe, to see what is and is not there, and to explore gently what people's motivations and reasons for acting are. You formulate theories based on the evidence all around you, which enable you to develop a sophisticated understanding of why something is happening. This is also useful for understanding and analysing spiritual abuse: what is there, who is behaving in what way, why they are doing something, why they are avoiding other things, and so on and so forth.

Third, the analysis of sacred texts is helpful. The Bible is both used to build people up and abused to break them down. Exploitative and coercive language around submission, obedience and claiming a direct connection to God are all regular features of spiritually abusive contexts. Conversations with people of other religious traditions make it clear that this is not uniquely a Christian problem. Rather, it is a problem that we all face and an issue we must all respond to. How do we ensure sacred texts are used to build people up and not to tear them down?

Who is this book for?

I have written this book to help people of different religious perspectives to understand and respond to the reality of spiritual abuse. Anglican Christians will perhaps get the most from this book, because I am writing as an Anglican who has a personal and professional interest in safeguarding. But I believe there is plenty to interest peoples of all religions and no religion, those who have a professional stake in safeguarding and those with more general concerns.

Abuse of religion and spirituality is rarely out of the news. Whether it concerns the case of Mike Pilavachi, Ravi Zacharias, Peter Ball, Jonathan Fletcher, John Smyth or an organization such as NXIUM, religion is twisted to harm the innocent. In many of my conversations with people of different religions, they recognize the reality of spiritual abuse but do not know what to do about it. I hope this book will play a small part in equipping people to respond.

INTRODUCTION: TRUST MATTERS

Some of what is written here may be difficult or distressing for you to read. If that is the case, I urge you to find practical support and help: https://www.actiononspiritualabuse.org.uk, https://safespacesenglandandwales.org.uk and https://inshaykhsclothing.com are all good places to seek support.

The structure of the book

The book is divided into four parts. First, there is some orientating information, explaining what is meant by spiritual abuse and introducing key words and phrases for discussion. Second, I provide the findings of my research, which involves going into detail about what people think about spiritual abuse and how best to respond to it. Third, there is reflection on the realities of spiritual abuse, which explores six Church of England cases of spiritual abuse, and develops a Christian theological approach to the issues. Fourth, I suggest some responses to the findings, including how we can build a more robust religious landscape. I also provide some case studies and scenarios that are designed to make you think about what exactly spiritual abuse is and is not, and how best to respond – whatever the situation.

PART I

Understanding

In Part I, I ask what is meant by the term 'spiritual abuse', using real-life examples from different religions. I also discuss the role of culture.

I

What Are We Talking About?

> From my experience I do not think that the idea of church being a safe place would be discussed when Jonathan was vicar. It was not a safe place for those who worked there – as those who were in the Emmanuel preaching groups might disclose – where people who were not up to the grade would be humiliated. (thirtyone:eight, 2021, p. 39)

Churches – or any religious institution – are not necessarily safe places. This chapter discusses what is meant by spiritual abuse, including whether it should be regarded as a specific category of abuse. I cover what I mean by 'spiritual abuse', discuss other definitions, give examples of abuse in different religions and explore the role of culture.

What do you mean by 'spiritual abuse'?

Although the term is never used in either the Hebrew Scriptures or the New Testament, you can find examples of what we would now call spiritual abuse. In Ezekiel 34, the Lord accuses the bad shepherds, the leaders of God's people, who have failed to care for God's people. The Lord sets out his accusation:

> You eat the fat, you clothe yourselves with the wool, you slaughter the fatlings; but you do not feed the sheep. You have not strengthened the weak, you have not healed the sick, you have not bound up the injured, you have not brought back the strayed, you have not sought the lost, but with force and harshness you have ruled them. (vv. 3–5)

The leaders were supposed to use their spiritual power and authority to care for the people. Instead, they were interested only in their own well-being.

In 1 Corinthians 8, Paul warns against using personal Christian knowledge to harm those believers who are less secure in their faith. This passage could be understood as a response to spiritual abuse.

But what is spiritual abuse? David Johnson and Jeff VanVonderen define spiritual abuse as 'the mistreatment of a person who is in need of help, support or greater spiritual empowerment, with the result of weakening, undermining or decreasing that person's spiritual empowerment' (Johnson and VanVonderen, 1991, p. 20). They explain that spiritual abuse occurs when a leader uses his or her spiritual position to the detriment of another. But it might not be just one person. They also explore the existence of spiritually abusive systems, the risks of posturing for positions of power, a performance-driven culture and a lack of balance (Johnson and VanVonderen, 1991, pp. 63–71). This definition is a good place to start, but is it clear enough? What do 'mistreatment' or 'spiritual empowerment' mean? Some further thinking is needed if we are to satisfy ourselves that spiritual abuse really exists.

Guidance from the Methodist Church defines spiritual abuse as 'coercion and control of one individual by another in a spiritual context' (Methodist Church, 2022, pp. 112–17, following Oakley and Kinmond, 2014). The Methodist guidance comes in a list of 'other forms of abuse', which are institutional abuse, domestic abuse, controlling behaviour, human trafficking, modern slavery, and abuse using social media and/or a mobile phone (Methodist Church, 2022, pp. 117–19).

The Church of England is clear both that 'spiritual abuse is often an integral element of other experiences of abuse within the Christian and other faith contexts', and that spiritual abuse should be categorized as a form of emotional and psychological abuse, especially when reporting such abuse to external agencies. The guidance states that, in a safeguarding context, spiritual abuse of children is emotional abuse, while spiritual abuse of adults is psychological abuse (Church of England, 2021, section

4.2.1). I think this is to make sure that there is no confusion in dealing with abuse, and that appropriate legal definitions are referred to when building a case for prosecution.

Does spiritual abuse happen?

The leading UK-based academic writer on spiritual abuse from a Protestant Christian perspective is Professor Lisa Oakley. She has been researching this topic for more than 15 years. Professor Oakley teamed up with Justin Humphreys of the safeguarding charity thirtyone:eight to write a book that summarizes the academic debate and research Oakley and others have conducted. They give the following detailed definition:

> Spiritual abuse is a form of emotional and psychological abuse. It is characterised by a systematic pattern of coercive and controlling behaviour in a religious context. Spiritual abuse can have a deeply damaging impact on those who experience it.
> This abuse may include manipulation and exploitation, enforced accountability, censorship of decision-making, requirements for secrecy and silence, coercion to conform, control through the use of sacred texts or teaching, requirement of obedience to the abuser, the suggestion that the abuser has a 'divine' position, isolation as a means of punishment, and superiority and elitism. (Oakley and Humphreys, 2019, p. 31)

The definition begins with a general categorization and statement of the impact of spiritual abuse, before offering a refined, non-exhaustive list of what spiritual abuse might look like. The reference to a 'systematic pattern' is important to ensure one-off mistakes are not classified as abuse. Notice the reference to 'sacred texts or teaching', not 'Scripture' and 'pulpit', which perhaps reflects a desire to develop a definition of spiritual abuse that is workable in multiple religions. By focusing on actions, it provides guidance for those who do not have a faith of their own. The definition can therefore be used by the authorities, such as the police and social services, in responding to reports of spiritual abuse. Professor Oakley has developed a robust and detailed definition of spiritual abuse. But that does not mean it has been universally accepted.

Some people think that we should not use the specific term 'spiritual abuse'. The Evangelical Alliance (EA) argues that it is better simply to refer to emotional or psychological harm occurring in a faith context (Evangelical Alliance, 2018, p. 1). The EA is worried about the risk of 'proto-legal mission creep': that is, a legal definition of spiritual abuse that damages freedoms of religious thought, expression and assembly (Evangelical Alliance, 2018, pp. 3–4). The EA argues that the term 'spiritual abuse' is counterproductive, especially because it 'too readily conflates *actions* and *effects* with *motivation, role* and *setting*' (Evangelical Alliance, 2018, p. 11). It argues that existing legislation related to psychological abuse provides sufficient scope for prosecution and conviction of any perpetrators, although personal experiences of abuse are not discussed (Evangelical Alliance, 2018, pp. 16–18). Its primary point is that 'spiritual abuse' is a dangerously vague term and is likely to do more harm than good.

The EA position is that existing legislation related to emotional and psychological abuse provides sufficient grounds for prosecution of the actions and effects. There is no need, therefore, to stray into questioning the motivation (which is hard to determine) and official role of any perpetrators, let alone including the setting in which abuse took place.

Arguably, recently introduced legislation on 'positions of trust' deals with the issue in a manner that reflects some of the EA's concerns. The provision of the Sexual Offences Act of 2003 has been extended to make it a criminal offense for someone in a 'position of trust' to engage in sexual activity with a person in their care who is aged 16 or 17. Religious leaders are included within the definition of 'position of trust'. This indicates the possibility of abuse that is primarily sexual but with an emotional or psychological aspect in a religious or spiritual context. On the legislative change, see Home Office (2022b), 'Positions of Trust'.

The EA has a point. It is certainly the case that many staff in organizations, such as the police, have little or no understanding of lived religion and belief, so there is a potential risk of inappropriately labelling actions or attitudes as spiritual abuse. Is it abuse to teach creationism, for example? Or to say that marriage should be between a man and a woman? Or to suggest sex outside marriage is wrong? Or to ask people to give ten per cent of their pre-tax income to their church?

I understand the concerns of the EA. But if 'spiritual abuse' is used primarily as an internal, catch-all term within a religious organization, then there is value in developing a much needed conversation about healthy cultures and supporting those who have suffered harm perpetrated in a faith context.

As I was reading around the topic, I discovered some research by psychologists that I found useful in formulating my understanding of spiritual abuse. David Ward refers to the 'phenomenon of spirituality that has turned toxic; that is, via a range of psychosocial processes, it ceases to be beneficial to the adherent, and instead becomes a tool to inflict psycho-spiritual damage' (Ward, 2011, p. 899). This is a helpful discussion starter. You can have an interesting conversation exploring what 'spirituality turned toxic' means. Donal Dorr gives an example. He was told that laughing at a dirty joke was a mortal sin, condemning him to hell for all eternity (Dorr, 2000, p. 527). Here, spirituality has ceased to be beneficial and has become damaging and toxic for the believer.

Ward interviewed six individuals to explore further the nature of this damage. He argues for six core themes of spiritual abuse:

1 the leadership represents God to those who are abused;
2 spiritual bullying, dictating standards of behaviour;
3 acceptance via (fear-based) performance;
4 spiritual neglect, that is, not responding to pastoral or practical needs;
5 an expanding tension between the desire to please the leadership (and God) and the desire for healthy human activities, such as expressing doubts or being comforted when in pain;
6 this internal tension manifests as ill health.

Even if you do not agree with the term 'spiritual abuse', you probably still recognize these as harmful behaviours. For me, the term spiritual abuse is primarily for use within religious organizations, to help them get their houses in order. Whether it is a useful term for the authorities to use is a separate issue. Chapter 7 discusses working with the authorities.

Ward concludes by defining spiritual abuse as a

> misuse of power in a spiritual context whereby spiritual authority is distorted to the detriment of those under its leadership. It is a multifaceted and multilayered experience that includes acts of commission and omission, aimed at producing conformity. It is both process and event, influencing one's inner and outer worlds and has the potential to affect the biological, psychological, social and spiritual domains of the individual. (Ward, 2011, p. 913)

This definition needs discussing. 'Authority' might be individual or institutional. There is no list of examples because every case is different. The reference to acts of omission (to leaving things out) is also useful, as it reminds us of the possibility of pastoral neglect as a form of spiritual abuse. Abuse is both ongoing and immediate. It has an impact on every aspect of an individual's life. This is important in the context of clinical and psychological support for those affected by spiritual abuse.

In workshops, I use a simple definition to stimulate conversation:

> Spiritual abuse takes place when an individual or group engages in coercive and controlling behaviour of others in a faith context. Religious beliefs and practices are used to justify behaviour and actions that are harmful to the victim. The victim of the abuse may not be aware that they are being abused.

All this reading and thinking has convinced me that spiritual abuse really does happen. Sometimes, it might be obvious, such as when a man uses a sacred text to justify raping his wife. But at other times, it can be hard to decide if 'spiritual abuse' is the right term. Did the sermon on financial giving cross the line into abuse or was it just unhealthy? Some concrete examples will help us to develop our thinking.

WHAT ARE WE TALKING ABOUT?

Spiritual abuse in different religious traditions

One researcher suggests five effects of spiritual abuse that are common across religious traditions (Fernández, 2022, p. 430). These are

1 a loss of freedom – a real state of slavery
2 a distortion of the image of God
3 undermining the systems of meaning making
4 the impact on the ability to trust in others and oneself
5 the construct of depression.

While there are commonalities, there are also features that are particular to a given religious tradition. Samuel Fernández gives the example that vulnerability is a condition of Christian discipleship. As a follower of Jesus, I make myself vulnerable to others who are in spiritual authority over me. This means that the institution of the Church is partially responsible for spiritual abuse perpetrated by anyone to whom the Church has given authority (Fernández, 2022, pp. 432–3).

Spiritual abuse within Jewish contexts is, in some senses, like abuse elsewhere. For example, the number of Orthodox Jewish women who reported sexual abuse was 'essentially the same as that reported in studies of the general population' (Blau, 2017, p. 50). Researchers identified three types of spiritual abuse perpetrated against women: belittling spiritual worth, beliefs or deeds; preventing the performance of spiritual acts; and causing transgression of spiritual obligations or prohibitions. Within a Jewish context, this included a husband mocking his wife's prayers, saying that they were of no spiritual value; not being allowed to buy ingredients to make challah, the special bread eaten on a Friday night to welcome the Sabbath; and forcing a wife to have sexual intercourse during her menstrual period (Dehan and Levi, 2009, pp. 1300–01). The specific actions are distinctive to Judaism, but these types of abuse could occur in other contexts.

The refusal to grant a divorce is another example. Within Judaism, 'the couple must mutually agree to end the marriage through the husband's giving and the wife's receiving a writ of

Jewish divorce, known as a *get'* (Starr, 2017, p. 43). If the *get* is not given, then the wife remains religiously married, even if she has completed civil divorce proceedings. This means she would be unable to remarry, because to do so would be regarded, from a religious perspective, as committing adultery. Moreover, any children from the second union would be considered illegitimate and hence unable to marry within Judaism (Starr, 2017, p. 43). While the specific example of *get*-refusal is particular to Judaism, a wife's decision to stay in an unhappy or abusive marriage and to submit to her husband, because of religious teaching, occurs in other religious traditions.

Finally, a team of academics researched Muslim experiences of abuse by religious authority figures. They identified two themes. These are toxic silence, when victims do not share their experience, and barriers to acknowledgement of abuse because no one will believe that a religious leader can do anything wrong (Chowdhury et al., 2021). Both phenomena occur in many religions.

Conversations on spiritual abuse are taking place in numerous religious contexts. Saffiyah Ally, a Muslim blogger, writes:

> Now and then we find ourselves reeling in shock at the news of a Sheikh or Imam who has abused their position of privilege and authority. Someone who manipulates, bullies and controls, uses religion for their personal gain, hurts vulnerable people, and doesn't seem to care. The sad thing is that these religious leaders are usually very well-liked and respected and people flock to them. People want to spend time in their company and they want to be like them. For many people, these religious leaders embody Islam and they might feel that if they get closer to them, they get closer to God. Many people might find themselves thinking that perhaps some of their faith, wisdom, and goodness will rub off on us. Instead, we feel confused and betrayed when we discover they aren't what they seem. (Ally, 2022)

This issue – of people with power being beyond criticism or challenge – is not unique to Islam. Sadly, it is all too common, but some religious leaders are responding to the problem. Dasa

(1999) gives a Hindu perspective. Sikh Women's Aid offers useful courses and support.

The role of culture

What is the role of culture within abuse? Culture is often defined simply as 'the way we do things around here'. If that way of behaving becomes toxic, then the impact can be devastating. The Independent Inquiry into Child Sexual Abuse found strong evidence that many faith-based groups do not have an organizational culture that takes safeguarding seriously (IICSA, 2021).

Professor Oakley worked with the Church of England Task and Finish Group to develop guidance on responding to the potential for spiritual abuse. They developed a continuum illustrating a spectrum of behaviour (see the diagram). The guidance gives detailed examples of behaviours that fit all four categories, of which one is discussed here.

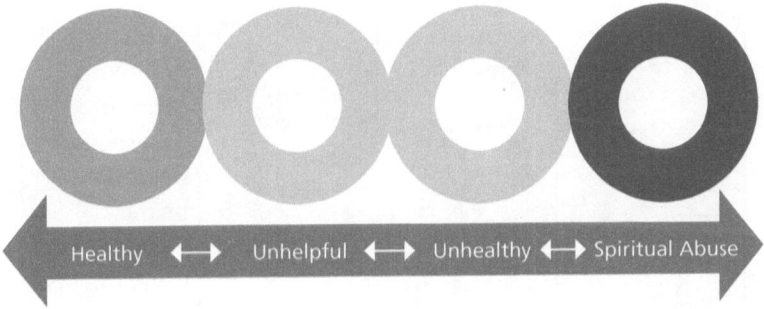

A spectrum of behaviour

Healthy ⟷ Unhelpful ⟷ Unhealthy ⟷ Spiritual Abuse

Table 1 uses the example of teaching on financial giving to highlight the distinctions between the categories. As is clear from the table, although the sample actions might be carried out by an individual, they will be both enabled and prohibited by organizational culture.

Table 1: Spectrum of behaviour: examples of the four categories of culture

Healthy culture	Unhelpful culture	Unhealthy culture	Spiritual abuse
Teaching about financial giving in a way that allows understanding of biblical passages and discipleship. Accepting that some will be more able than others to give financially.	Suggesting that most people could give more if they managed their finances more effectively. Being overly defensive when speaking to someone who has a different opinion from you on tithing.	Pressuring individuals or groups into financial giving. Giving more attention to individuals who are able to give financially. Developing a pattern of defensive and critical conversations with individuals who are unable to give financially.	Consistent, intrusive, coercive requests for financial giving, suggesting that the level of giving is the most important measure of the individual's commitment to God. The use of biblical Scripture persistently to coerce financial giving or using threats of spiritual consequences to invoke fear if finance is not provided.

WHAT ARE WE TALKING ABOUT?

Spiritual abuse does happen

Spiritual abuse is complex. It is therefore difficult to develop an all-encompassing definition. But at least seven points can be noted.

1. Spiritual abuse occurs in a faith-focused context when religion or spirituality cease to be supportive and become toxic.
2. It can be perpetrated by systems as well as individuals who may or may not have a position of hierarchical power, and who may or may not intend harm.
3. Spiritual abuse is both process and event: the impact of multiple incidents over time.
4. Spiritual abuse involves misuse of power for coercion and control, which manifests in a variety of ways, founded on the abuser taking a divine position over the abused.
5. It has a traumatic, complex and multilayered impact on individuals.
6. I have concentrated on personal experiences of abuse, with little or no exploration of the motivation and experience of perpetrators, nor of ways of preventing abuse.
7. While some do not accept the term 'spiritual abuse', even those critics wish to ensure that people are able to worship safely, without harm to themselves or others.

While you may still have reservations, hopefully I have persuaded you that spiritual abuse really does happen. The next step is to discuss another part of my research: what other people say about spiritual abuse.

PART II

Conversations

This section contains three chapters. In 'Conversations about Spiritual Abuse', I share findings from conversations with people across various religions about spiritual abuse. I share the patterns that emerged, from the role of toxic leaders to how we can better support those affected.

In 'Responses of Different Religions', I discuss the perspectives of different traditions on spiritual abuse, noting differences on the surface and underlying commonalities.

In 'The Power of Choice and Learning', I ask what gives us the power to resist spiritual abuse. Two themes emerged from the conversations: agency and education. In this chapter, I explore how these tools can help individuals and communities to protect themselves and create lasting change.

2

Conversations about Spiritual Abuse

> Any critique must start with ourselves; we need to remove our log before our brother's speck. This is not a problem 'out there' but 'in here'. (Stirling, 2023, p. xiii)

We need to talk about abuse if we are to make religious institutions safe. During my research, I spoke with 26 people about spiritual abuse. I have combined insights from all the conversations to write this chapter and Chapter 3. Here, there is a thematic focus, while Chapter 3 discusses spiritual abuse from different religious perspectives.

In this chapter, I explore why spiritual abuse is a distinct category of abuse, which anyone can perpetrate or experience. I discuss Lisa Oakley's continuum and how to reduce the risk of harm. The purpose here is to demonstrate that anyone can think about and respond to the issues. It will also help you to develop appropriate language for conversations about spiritual abuse.

Spiritual abuse is a distinct category of abuse

Most of those I talked with agreed that spiritual abuse is a distinct form of abuse. As one person explained:

> [Calling it spiritual abuse] tells you where it's happening and what it is and who it's between ... I can view spiritual, the word 'spiritual', as an environment in which this abuse has taken place. The word spiritual might also indicate a certain kind of relationship that only the spiritual environment would give access to, in order for that abuse to happen.

It is important to remember the abuser might not know that what they are doing is abusive. Someone referred to unwitting or unthinking racism as another example of unintentional poor practice. Equally, those who are abused may not be aware of their own victimization.

Participants gave specific examples of spiritual abuse, such as the use of Scripture for coercive control or manipulation and the inducement of guilt for failure to follow religious practice. Some abusers 'divinify control' of other people; for example, those who claim to be faith healers and deploy exploitative practices. One person said that spiritual abuse is

> when you divinify control, [you] divinify an abusive nature. So ... that's treating somebody badly or making them subservient, submissive. Making them give up things that they don't necessarily want to give up, whether that's physical, mental, or financial. And it can be a very fine line between mentoring somebody and spiritually abusing somebody.

Some saw spiritual abuse as a distinct category that had clear overlaps with either sexual or financial abuse. A person who had experienced abuse said:

> I think they can overlap, so we have different terms for things like physical abuse, emotional abuse and mental abuse. Well, it includes those things. It's a very different dynamic, where the power aspect is rooted in that belief or system that has ideas of God or power and hierarchy within it. I think that it can be a very particular kind of abuse, particularly using things like what sacred texts say sometimes. But also, I think, from my own experience, spiritual abuse is very different to, say, sexual abuse. It doesn't mean that the two can't inform each other.

The example of faith healers is relevant here, with reference made to individuals demanding payments or sexual favours to ensure the health of either those they are manipulating or their close family.

One person found it difficult to decide if there was a particular category of spiritual abuse. The point was made that different religions and, moreover, different people within a particular religion would draw the line in different places. How does one ensure objectivity, impartiality and fair treatment of everybody? The question of subjectivity and personal experience is one I will return to in Chapter 3.

A small minority of respondents had concerns like those expressed by the Evangelical Alliance. One person suggested spiritual abuse is only useful as a category if the definition helped with finding a solution to the problem. Another person was clear that spiritual abuse is not a useful category, primarily because it is difficult or even impossible to measure and report accurately. Concern was raised particularly over the ignorance of the authorities (the police and social services) in understanding how faith communities function, and the risk of abuse being compounded by ham-fisted responses. Two people talked about people losing and recovering their faith. An individual might experience spiritual abuse and need spiritual support in coming to terms with their experience and potentially returning to a position of faith.

Finally, some participants argued that everybody is spiritual whether they are religious or not. Is there a sense in which all abuse is spiritual in that all abuse goes to the core of human beings' identity?

Abusers and the abused

If spiritual abuse is a distinct category of abuse, how should we refer to those who abuse and those who are abused? One participant suggested that 'anybody who has a position of trust and influence that is predicated upon a religious idea' has the potential to abuse. Another person agreed:

> I think anyone has the potential to be a perpetrator, and anybody has the potential to be abused. I'm certainly aware of my own power that I have within my own institution, and I have also been on the receiving end of different forms of abuse within my own context as well.

There are questions of intentionality. While some may seek power so they can abuse people, others are corrupted by power and slip into abusive practices. People in this latter group

> may incrementally recognize over time that they have influence and, over time, maybe lose sight of that which the faith teaches, and they become enamoured in their own power, and almost become God-like themselves ... And I think there's a real danger of that.

The danger is that without grounding in a religious community, people of influence believe their own hype and presume a status that is not theirs to hold. There are also questions of cognition and self-awareness, related both to those who abuse and those who experience abuse. Do they have the mental capacity to understand their own actions and experiences? If not, does it matter what label is used to define those experiences?

Those who abuse might be called the 'abuser' or 'perpetrator' or 'the accused'. Other labels mentioned were

- wolf in sheep's clothing
- protagonist
- religious leader
- anyone.

This final label, mentioned by only a few people, is a warning to all of us to pay attention to how we use the power that we have. As one participant explained:

> But spiritual abuse isn't always them [religious leaders]. And this is the key thing, and I think this is a dangerous mistake to make where you think the person doing the abusing is going to be this way or this way, or they will have this quality. A spiritual abuser could be anyone, just simply someone who knows how to prey on someone vulnerable and prey on their weakness. It could be your grandma. It could be someone in the family. It could be anyone.

What about those who experience abuse? For some participants, 'victim' and 'survivor' could be used interchangeably; but most suggested it was important for those who are abused to describe themselves in ways they are comfortable with. We do not want to help people recover from experiences of coercive control by controlling how they define their experiences. But at the same time, I recognize that 'victim' is a potentially negative self-definition. One participant noted the risk that defining oneself as a victim can reduce agency. By contrast, another participant suggested that 'survivor' has 'connotations of hope and aspiration'.

One person noted that some of those who have been abused refer to themselves as 'thrivers', suggesting that they have overcome the negative impact of the abuse they have experienced. Perhaps children, who are especially vulnerable, should be defined as victims rather than survivors of abuse.

A participant who had experienced abuse argued that those who are abused experience a

> point of suicidal, loneliness, darkness, spiritual confusion, constant anxiety, fluctuation of hyper-anxiety, mild anxiety. But there's a sense of uneasiness throughout this whole kind of period.

As I thought about what I had heard, I recognized the importance of empowerment and agency, whether for those who are abused or for those at risk of abuse, which in practice means all people of faith. If a key aspect of spiritual abuse is coercive control, then a central element of resistance will be individual and corporate agency: the ability to say no to inappropriate labels, actions and requests.

The continuum

Discussion of Lisa Oakley's continuum for defining organizational cultures, from healthy through unhelpful to unhealthy and, finally, to spiritual abuse, was enlightening and enriching. It is an excellent tool for starting discussions about the nature and impact of spiritual abuse. As a participant explained, 'I would say, without any hesitation, this is very helpful ... it captures the different levels that I have already seen, you know, being manifested in churches.'

One participant noted the speed of deterioration of a relationship from healthy to unhealthy. Decisive action stopped things getting any worse, but the change took only a few weeks. Building on the point about agency made above, it is crucial that people of faith are aware of the early, seemingly harmless, stages of the grooming process, so they are better equipped to resist the seduction of the abuser. As another participant put it:

> Now, without those kinds of checks and balances to individuals or groups, what begins, as you know, very passionate and committed faithfulness can move into the unhelpful, the unhealthy and toward spiritual abuse. Everything can move in that direction. And I would say it begins with that sense of when people lose connection with that, the wider community or the wider knowledge base.

A participant noted the risk of 'false safety'. You might conduct DBS checks, have and follow a safer recruitment policy and a low-level concerns policy, and so forth. But these precautions will not mean abuse cannot take place. While a culture of vigilance is important, one can never say never and must always be aware of the awful possibility that abuse might be happening.

Finally, the continuum proved a useful tool for exploring what abuse looks like in different religious contexts: a point discussed in more detail in Chapter 3. One participant suggested the continuum was useful when combined with examples, such as around money. The participant added, 'I think it is always a good way of introducing the topic, because I think you create relatability to personal experience and [the] people who are involved.' They suggested another example was around 'personal responsibility'; that is,

> the responsibility of practising your faith, and actually what you should be doing, or what you want to do rather than having one's personal spiritual practices dictated by other people, including faith leaders.

This confirms my finding both in research and in practical workshops that the continuum is an excellent way of giving people a language and means of categorizing their own experience.

What can leaders do to reduce the risk of harm?

This section is aimed especially at leaders. The strongest themes that emerged from this section of the conversations were those of education and empowerment, and of awareness and accountability. I have grouped the responses about reducing the risk of harm into six main categories:

1 safeguarding policies and procedures
2 involving external agencies
3 empowering individuals
4 peer accountability
5 community culture change
6 training and education.

Safeguarding policies and procedures

Policies and procedures are the foundations of safeguarding. They must be produced and owned by the leaders of the religious organization. Paperwork downloaded from the Internet or produced by AI will have no meaningful impact on behaviour or culture. In fact, it might give a false sense of security and so be worse than having no policy at all.

One participant discussed three areas of work: safer recruitment; policies and procedures; and training. The participant pointed out that all three needed to be implemented properly for them to be effective. The participant also raised the issue of working with volunteers; they noted that with employees, these actions can easily be made mandatory; but when working with volunteers in a faith context, soft power and a motivational approach are required. The participant indicated that the most effective way of reducing risk is to make it hard for abuse to take place, for example by ensuring that no one is alone with vulnerable people.

Involving external agencies

Religious communities should not act in isolation; they should involve external agencies in the right way, at the right time. One participant suggested that the police have a role in educating people about their rights and the nature of the proof needed to bring a criminal conviction for abuse. Another participant proposed the possibility of external audits of faith community groups. The participant recognized the technical challenges in providing people with suitable skills to conduct such audits effectively; but they argued that audits would provide an important element of accountability. The participant also suggested schools have a role to play in educating children and young people about the risks of spiritual abuse.

Many participants were cautious about the involvement of the authorities (the police and social services). Several participants stipulated that they had to be trained.

One participant added:

> People in Leicester organizations, particularly any sort of community faith-type organizations now know the authorities, government, local government, police can't do anything to them. There's almost like a carte blanche to do what you want. Because it's so easy to play the race card, the religion card, the victim card.

Of course, this issue is not unique to Leicester. Another person was also cautious:

> It seems such a long way away from having a statutory agency involved because it's so subtle ... how do you bring in a statutory agency that's dealing with, actually, people's deep, deep rooted, well, beliefs and spirituality?

Someone else said, 'I suppose that comes down to the agencies and their ability to recognize the differences in different aspects of the faith.'

But however cautious or concerned religious people are about external agencies, they cannot ignore them. As numerous cases have shown, not going to the authorities results in abuse continuing unchecked. As one participant explained:

> I think such agencies have some role. What I am not sure about is when. Because I think, also, the authorities can bring their own problems in the way that they deal with issues. So, some issues may become magnified. Some issues may be seen out of context of their local community dynamics. Some things may just be misunderstood. Sometimes, when something's handed over to the law, an issue that could have quite easily been resolved becomes fixed, and then it becomes, you know, irreconcilable.

External agencies should be involved in responding to spiritual abuse. The tough questions are exactly when and how.

Empowering individuals

We must equip people to respond proactively to the possibility of spiritual abuse: as a participant proposed, 'People standing up for issues where they see dangerous power dynamics and having the courage to call that out.' Or as someone else put it: 'Raising awareness ... letting people know that it's not a shameful thing to seek for help and to let them know that the support systems are out there.' Those who experience abuse feel powerless and isolated. We should ensure that they are accompanied and empowered to act.

One person suggested a four-stage process of awareness, alertness, attention and action:

> [You] say to somebody, are you aware of what is happening? Are you of aware of the distress and the confusion which is

being caused by you? ... Are you alert to yourself as to what is the dynamic which is going on? Paying attention to it? Because this is something which is going to be harmful for you. And then take action – because you can reduce this risk by not listening to this person, not being in the same environment, not being in the same structure as this person – and to remove yourself, and find other ways of expressing your own kind of religious and spiritual beliefs, without getting abused or manipulated.

These four As of awareness, alertness, attention and action are similar to my ideas about agency and education; they provide a useful framework that complements the continuum discussed on pp. 17–18.

Accountability

Anyone who has spiritual authority should be held appropriately accountable. One person proposed that 'any spiritual adviser should have somebody above him or her whom he or she is accountable to'. Someone else argued for dialogue and accountability, proposing a person 'like a "duty supervisor", who can actually resolve these kind of issues'. Ministers of religion often have enormous freedom to determine how they use their time. When this is done well, it is a real blessing to their religious communities. But, as the Church of England case studies discussed in Chapter 5 show, unaccountable individuals can cause tremendous damage. As a participant explained, 'I think it's time we educate, and we put the spotlight [on to show] that, actually, hold on a minute, this can happen, but also hold people accountable, especially faith leaders.' No one should work entirely in isolation.

Community culture change

As several participants argued, the possibility of spiritual abuse must be discussed more openly in faith-based organizations. But how can we bring about cultural change? One participant argued that there is currently a cultural shift underway about the importance of talking about and acting with regard to safeguarding. There is a greater openness and willingness to talk about these issues. Abuse is no longer the taboo subject it once was, although in many communities there are still significant cultural and social barriers to be overcome. There is a significant need to unpack the power dynamics within religious communities. Those that have a hierarchical structure embed differences in status and power that can be easily abused. How can appropriate structures exist without providing opportunities for the abuse of power?

We must avoid responding to coercive control with coercive control of our own. Cultural change is a subtle and complex process that takes time, energy and resources. In some very hierarchical religious contexts (for example, the Church of England), superficial cultural change can be imposed in a top-down fashion. The question remains as to how effective and deep rooted such changes are. Some other religious groupings do not have any sort of hierarchy, but operate under much flatter structures. As a participant said:

> People can hide behind informality. But the good thing about that is that when you do identify something, and you find something going wrong, it is then easier to change because you're not talking about a massive infrastructure change. It is often one or two people who are setting that culture. And if you can change them, the culture also changes. So, the informality can then work in your favour. So, at times, I think the informality will work against us [but], at times, it will work in our favour. And that's just the reality of what we have to live with.

I agree with the participant who said, 'Creating a culture that educates, then empowers is probably the right order in which to do things.' Cultural change is crucial for tackling spiritual abuse, but incredibly difficult to do, especially if the congregation is not interested in or is opposed to change. Although much good work has been done in dealing with spiritual abuse, there remains a lot more to do.

Training and education

There is a need for more preventative measures, such as religiously and culturally appropriate awareness programmes, toolkits, and signposting people towards assistance. Moreover, if people have greater understanding and grounding in their faith, they are more likely to call out abusive practices. Education is a central element of attempts to reduce the risk of spiritual abuse.

The nature of this education must be carefully considered. Survivor testimonies have an important part to play but are not enough in and of themselves. Creative education methods would have a greater impact. In pastoral supervision, supervisors will often use what are termed 'projective methods' to enable the supervisee to step outside an issue and view it with greater objectivity. Photographs, poetry, short stories and even drama may be helpful ways of explaining the impact of spiritual abuse. There's more on this in Chapter 8.

But will we learn from the past? Some participants thought people would, especially those who were not aware that what they were doing was wrong. Others were unsure. But, a participant said, 'If you want to learn from past mistakes, look at what happened from the early stages and not just the final events.' Someone else suggested that learning from the past will happen only if people are held accountable for delivering the recommendations of lessons-learned reviews. The sad reality is that many never-again situations happen far too often.

We should recognize the reality that lay leaders within congregations are often untrained and, therefore, may knowingly or unknowingly abuse power. Hence appropriate training is vital. Bystander programmes are effective only when skills and knowledge are empowering people. We should focus on the empowerment of groups of individuals: this is too much for one person on their own.

Support for leaders

The final area explored in the conversations was whether pastoral supervision or any other interventions had a role to play in reducing the risk of spiritual abuse. The overwhelming majority of participants felt that pastoral supervision might be useful but only if suitable accountability measures were in place. As one participant put it, there is a need for both 'carrot and stick'. It was noted by some that even a rigorous process such as pastoral supervision could be 'gamed'; that is, there is a risk of false compliance. There are at least three aspects to the support: appropriate institutional accountability, personal development and peer support.

Pastoral supervision would be effective provided it included appropriate accountability. For this to work, those in positions of hierarchical responsibility, where such positions exist, must take the risk of abuse seriously. Faith-based organizations cannot just leave people to get on with things as they see fit. Those concerned need to move towards much greater organized care and support for one another. There is a need for trusted, well-grounded, well-balanced, trained individuals who are in positions to be able to provide supervision.

At the same time, people need to develop individual decision-making capacity, rather than relying too much on every detail of their lives being directed by a religious leader. Supervision should be combined with self-understanding; those in leadership must be aware of their own weaknesses and failings. One participant argued that leaders must be 'streetwise', in the sense of recognizing the risks and potential for abuse to occur.

Finally, there is a need for peer mentoring, and safe spaces where problems can be explored and where appropriate continuing professional development is provided. These would include safeguarding courses and helplines. Peer support could be given both by colleagues, with more experience than you, and closed Facebook groups and other similar social media discussion forums that enable people to raise issues and receive support, guidance and advice from their peers. Alternatively, leaders could have mentor and intra- and inter-faith community dialogues on spiritual abuse.

The key point raised in this section is the need for cultural change, including helping people, especially faith leaders who have been recruited from overseas, to appropriate the British understanding of safeguarding and how religious organizations run in this country.

As I listened, I began thinking in terms of agency and education. Leaders are equipped, through pastoral supervision and other tools, to embrace their own agency and care for themselves. But there is also external accountability to ensure compliance, which indicates the agency of congregation members. Through the education of newly arrived faith leaders, they, and their followers, are also given agency to live successful, faith-filled lives in the UK.

Learn and act

The key themes that emerged from my conversations were agency and education: A&E, if you like. We must be alert to the awful possibility that spiritual abuse might be taking place in our religious groups. As one participant noted, a situation can swiftly deteriorate from being healthy to unhelpful, and from there to unhealthy or even abusive. Everyone in faith-based organizations must have the appropriate agency to act. The four As framework of awareness, alertness, attention and action provides a suitable guide for what forms such agency could take.

Several people indicated their lack of understanding of the detail of spiritual abuse. This means it is important to conduct informal education programmes. These would include some study of perpetrators' motivations or grooming techniques but focus primarily on learning to be alert and aware: a cultural shift that enables open and honest discussion of the possibility of spiritual abuse. As some participants noted, it is difficult to come up with an all-encompassing definition of what is and what is not spiritual abuse. As someone said, it might occur in a 'very sweet, happy environment'. Education would therefore have to be scenario- or case-study based, facilitating discussion concerning practice, ensuring appropriate procedures are in place, and equipping people to resist those who seek to abuse the authority and power they have gained through their positions within religious organizations. The focus is not on developing a detailed definition but on empowering action.

A related point is the cost of speaking out. Several focus group participants noted there is always a risk in challenging inappropriate, unhealthy and abusive behaviour. However well an investigation is managed, however carefully a process is conducted, it is unlikely to remain confidential; those who speak out are likely to experience pushback. Whistleblowers will always pay a price for doing what is right. Such individuals are faced with an awful choice. Do they stay and experience the hostility of their peers? Or do they leave and lose the community of which they are part? *Call Me Evil, Let Me Go*, a pseudonymous account of experiencing and leaving a spiritually abusive Christian context, documents this dilemma in painful detail (Jones, 2011). Agency can come with a cost.

Religious organizations must recognize both their privileged position and their consequent responsibility for the care and well-being of those who attend their gatherings and learn from their leaders. Religious organizations also have a responsibility to care for those in leadership and positions of authority. Pastoral supervision, adequately resourced and appropriately enforced, was recognized by the participants as one possible means of doing this. Good mentors, supportive peers and a culture that allows questions and doubts to emerge are also key components. The possibility of false compliance must also be recognized. Those who abuse work hard to groom not only their victims but also their congregations and those with oversight responsibility. The well-documented case of the Church of England bishop Peter Ball is a clear example of this problem (IICSA, 2019). Those in positions of leadership in faith communities would do well to learn from the mistakes of the past.

3

Responses of Different Religions

Spiritual abuse happens when a leader with spiritual authority uses that authority to coerce, control or exploit followers, thus causing spiritual wounds. (Blue, 1993, p. 12).

Spiritual abuse can potentially take place in any spiritual context. This chapter explores three specific issues: the responses of different religions; the question of subjectivity in defining spiritual abuse, with examples from different religions; and cultural competence. I have recounted the thoughts of those interviewed in some detail to show that spiritual abuse is possible in many different religious traditions.

From my conversations with participants of different religions, it appears that there are superficial differences in the form that spiritual abuse takes but the underlying similarities are striking. I have listed the religions in alphabetical order.

Christian

Christian participants referred to the dangers of theological teaching as a grounding or foundation for spiritual abuse. The specific examples given were teaching on the role of women, teaching about the devil and the demonic, and teaching about 'conversion therapy' in relation to LGBT+ people. Where is the line between legitimate theological opinion and spiritual abuse?

A second issue was the risk of undue deference, characterized for example in the Anglo-Catholic tradition of Anglicanism as 'Father knows best'. This type of clericalism takes different forms in different theological strands of Christianity or in different religions. But the underlying problem remains the same. A related point concerned ministerial freedom. If clergy are largely free to determine their own timetable and workload, how do you introduce appropriate accountability?

Third, the question of false compliance with any accountability regime, such as pastoral supervision, was also raised. Many Christian churches have made great progress in introducing both safeguarding training and appropriate accountability mechanisms for clergy, but there is much work still to be done. It is important to balance autonomy with accountability. How can people in leadership positions become agents of their own well-being?

Hindu

The main concern raised by Hindu participants is typified by the description of abuse as 'divinified control'. The perpetrators might be termed 'false gurus', whose actions stunt rather than facilitate the personal growth of their disciples. One Hindu referred to the risk of mentoring crossing the line into abuse, which might be financial or sexual, or it might just be that the false guru was working for personal gain, not to give back. Another referred to coercive control of religious observance, whereby the false guru claims his way is the only way.

A second area of discussion was the abuse of power within mandir (temple) hierarchy, notably in the committee structure. Reference was made to those who had longstanding positions of power dictating what could or could not take place in a mandir; they would base their decisions more on their personal preferences rather than on any Hindu teaching. This type of abuse of power is masked by theological reasoning.

Third, one participant discussed the difficulty of whistleblowing. In a tight-knit community, where many people have known each other and worked together for decades, it can be very difficult to raise concerns about a senior religious leader, or even about one of the guru's disciples. Those who do raise concerns are sometimes ostracized and attacked. This is a cultural issue, not dissimilar to the 'Father knows best' mentality discussed in the previous section.

Fourth, for one participant, an abuser is 'anyone that the victim puts in a position of trust'. Concerning the abused, the participant recognized that some people are victims, but that others knowingly engage with people who are not credible. The participant explained:

> So, there can be lots of people like, you know, sometimes you park your car in certain areas, and you get these little fliers stuck on your car window: 'I can solve your marriage problems', 'I can solve your financial problems', 'Ring this number'.

The point is that people may knowingly engage in risky behaviour. They may, for example, recognize that the flyer advertising immediate solutions to financial problems is a scam that puts them at risk of financial abuse in a spiritual context. But that knowledge does not stop them ringing the number. To further illustrate the point, the participant gave the example of lemons used in Hindu tantric rituals. Lemons are 'imbued with my bad luck [and] I place it at a crossroads (just before Diwali). When you drive over it, the bad luck/karma transfers to you.' The participant added:

> How can agencies deal with it? How can you tell people what to do? Where can they go to for help? What sort of terminology [do you] use to actually understand what spiritual abuse is? Because, you have to realize, if someone's being spiritually abused, to them, they might say, 'No, this isn't abuse. This is what should be happening. Because this is what I'm told should happen' ... That's where these spiritual abuses come in. I will give you this lemon, and I've made it powerful by chanting mantras on it. So, you now have to put it over whoever's done it, and just throw it in the crossroads ... I'm transferring your bad luck, or your bad spirits, or your bad energy, or whatever has happened to you to somebody else. So, your problem's solved ... And the reason it's on a crossroads? Because under Hindu tantric practices crossroads are seen as centres of energy, and that's why they're there.

The tantric properties of lemons was not what I expected to discuss when trying to define the abuser and the abused. But I have included the long quotation here because it illustrates the dilemma in defining abuser and abused. What exactly is abusive about this practice? Is it wrong? Why? Who (if anyone) is harmed by the practice? Does it matter?

Jewish

For several Jewish participants, inducing guilt at the failure of Torah observance, and/or manipulation to prevent observance, was a clear example of spiritual abuse. This might refer to enforcing what clothing is worn or suggestions that failing to observe kosher food laws could result in exclusion from the Jewish community or some form of divine punishment. It was striking that greater reference was made to spiritual abuse within a family context by the Jewish participants than by any other group. This might be because significant portions of Jewish faith and practice are based at home. A specific example was that of challah, plaited bread that must be baked in preparation for the observance of Shabbat (the Sabbath). Eating challah on a Friday evening is part of welcoming in Shabbat. A husband might prevent his wife from baking the bread and then berate her for her failure to observe Torah: a double form of abuse.

Two other examples were discussed. First, *get* refusal: that is, refusal by a husband to grant his wife a *get* – religious permission to divorce. This is a clear example of coercive control, whereby a religious practice is abused. Second, limiting educational opportunities, and hence life chances, by allowing children only to attend a yeshiva, a religious school. The main concern was that young people who experienced such a narrow education would be unequipped for life in twenty-first-century Britain.

One Jewish participant talked at length about the danger of victimhood as one's primary identity. Reference was made to the Holocaust and the importance of a more positive self-understanding, such as that of being a survivor rather than a victim. The point was not to belittle such experiences but, rather, to keep the Holocaust from being the primary or only means by which a person formed their identity. Thinking of yourself, or your ancestor, as a survivor of the Holocaust would allow for a positive world-view and approach to life.

Muslim

Muslim participants discussed how people might move away from faith because of spiritual abuse. Could such people eventually return to a form of faith if they wanted to? And if they did wish to practise their faith, how could they be helped to do so? Is there space within Islam for appropriate critical enquiry into the teachings of the faith? All the Muslim participants referred to the use of scripture or personal authority for coercive control and the lack of critical-thinking skills among those who were abused. One example given was teaching about what happens after death, with the threat of eternal damnation in hell for those who were disobedient. How should such teaching be responded to? The primary concern was to develop critical-thinking skills, so that individual Muslims could challenge inappropriate teaching whenever they heard it.

There was also discussion of financial or sexual elements of spiritual abuse, especially when people who set themselves up as faith/spiritual healers preyed on the vulnerable. These individuals might be termed 'false healers'. They claim to be able to ensure recovery from illness using folk remedies, which must be paid for in cash or through sexual favours. This is a further example of coercive control.

One Muslim participant gave a detailed example of how a group or individual might inadvertently cross the line into unhealthy and then abusive behaviour:

> I think you can get carried away, particularly if it's a group identity that you've bought into, you know. It's one thing if you're on your own. I mean, I think there are some forms of abuse that are quite clear. So, for example, if you're singled out and, let's say, there's a gender dynamic. There's a sexual

dynamic that I think is a clear thing to identify, whereas a broader type of spiritual abuse [is] where it's just coercion. It's [being] made to feel bad about their religion, bad about their own sense of attachment, or people playing on their guilt to manipulate them. But I think it is a lot more difficult to discern, you know, positive from negative; from normative behaviour to abusive behaviour. I think [it's] very difficult and especially if the whole congregation is in for the ride. And you've got, you know, four or five people within your group or, say, the majority of your group are all very keen to go down that route. You don't want to be left out. You don't want to be the person who's sort of saying, 'Oh, I'm not. I'm a bit uncomfortable with this,' because it makes you look a little bit, you know, wet. So I think it would be quite difficult in those sorts of circumstances to identify [abuse]. And what I was going to say is, even the person doing the abusing may not see that as abuse. They may see this as, 'Well I'm just trying to get the best out of my congregation. I want them to be closer to God. I want them to fulfil their potential in the best way possible. Why wouldn't I want them to receive the highest rewards in Paradise? And that means us having just a very strong clear yardstick. In the end, this is free. If they don't want to, they don't have to. I'm not forcing anybody. This is not coercive in the conventional sense.' They might not see it as coercive and so they may even push back and say, 'No, this is not abuse at all.' They may be fully convinced of that.

As this long quotation indicates, defining what spiritual abuse is can be highly subjective. I will return to this question below.

Sikh

Sikh participants referred to false teaching to enable coercive control, sexual abuse and financial exploitation. Several made specific reference to the grooming of individuals for abuse. The perpetrators could be described as 'false saints' who say to their followers, 'If you do not follow my teaching, God will punish you.' These false saints set themselves up as sole mediators of access to the divine. One Sikh participant noted that it is not necessarily the false saint who perpetrates the abuse; his followers may do so for him, either through aggressive policing of the group of devotees or by how they treat those who are outside the chosen circle.

Reference was also made to division and argument within families and the community; and false saints drawing people away from the Panth (community of Sikhs). This not only divides the community, it also makes it very difficult for those who have been abused to admit what has happened to them and return to active membership of the community. The challenge of responding appropriately to this issue is compounded by the fact that Sikhi (Sikhism) is a non-hierarchical faith. There is collective and communal decision-making, rather than a top-down command structure. As such, it can be potentially harder to weed out false saints.

Several Sikhs discussed the question of agency, responsibility to report spiritual abuse, and the empowerment of those who experience abuse. What does it mean to have agency in an abusive and/or toxic culture? Do those who experience abuse have genuine agency in the choices they make? Turning to the issue of financial abuse, if somebody takes out a loan or remortgages their house to provide funds to give to a 'false saint', were they coerced or did they make a free choice? They may have signed the relevant paperwork, apparently of their own volition, but the nature of the relationships they are caught up in will, perhaps, mean they did not do so of their own free will.

Spiritual abuse is similar in all religions

While the precise form that the spiritual abuse takes may differ from faith to faith, the underlying issues are similar. This strengthens the case for an interfaith approach to education about spiritual abuse, as people can learn from the experiences of those outside of their own faith community. Two common threads – of unaccountable individuals, who might be leaders, and of groomed or complicit congregations – emerged from my analysis of the interviews. The extreme examples are obvious. But what about the grey areas? The situations that are not clear cut are the real concern. Agency and education are key to resolving these issues.

You say it was spiritual abuse; I say it was helpful

Individual experience is subjective. For some people, a spiritual practice may be healthy, while others may find it unhelpful or even unhealthy. To give one example, consulting with one's guru about a minor decision might be a healthy spiritual practice to some but for others would be an unhelpful indication of unnecessary accountability. An overtly abusive practice may be obvious, but the situation is not always clear cut. Practices that seem sensible at a particular moment in time may, with hindsight, be revealed as abusive or at least inappropriate.

A good example of the issue of subjectivity is found in the Fletcher Review, which is discussed in detail in Chapter 5. The reviewers document the normalization of Jonathan Fletcher's spiritually abusive and bullying behaviour (thirtyone:eight, 2021, pp. 38, 53). As an unhealthy and spiritually abusive culture developed, those who had themselves been victims of Fletcher's abuse became abusers (thirtyone:eight, 2021, p. 68). While Fletcher may have been intentional in his actions, it is unlikely that those who experienced abuse at his hands set out to become abusers. Rather, they developed a warped sense of what was normal and simply enacted what they experienced. Those who are external to such a situation might expect people immediately to challenge unhealthy and spiritually abusive behaviour. But those who are being abused may not have sufficient agency to do so. As is often noted in domestic abuse situations, the abused may take a long time to recognize the reality of their situation and develop the courage to speak out or to leave.

One participant was clear that there are limits to subjectivity in defining abuse. They said:

> I think [it's] anything done knowingly, with the intention that you're not the qualified person for it. But you're abusing; you're profiting from someone's ill fortune. You're profiting from someone's down period. You're profiting from someone's, say, low mental health. That is abuse.

There are limits to subjectivity. Not everything is open to debate. Some behaviour may be merely unhelpful or unhealthy, but other behaviour is objectively and categorically abusive.

A Jewish participant argued that there is a generational shift underway, which is partly about different understandings of authority, partly about greater emphasis on well-being, and partly about whether we have a right not to be offended. There is therefore a risk of labelling unhealthy or unhelpful behaviour as abusive, as well as a risk of failure to challenge inappropriate behaviour out of a desire not to offend.

A Muslim participant commented that the notion of subjectivity resonated with their personal experience. The individual elaborated:

> And over the years, particularly the last ten years or so, I have had discussions with people who used to be involved at various points, and then we've departed paths ... moved away from each other. We have spoken about what we experienced in the early years, and we've disagreed. So, some, you know, one of us have said, oh, that was a very negative thing that we went through. And the other person has said no, that was a very positive thing, and it changed my life for the better. And that's two people going through exactly the same experience.

A Christian participant agreed that there was a degree of subjectivity in determining whether a particular action or practice was abusive or not.

> You need – we need – resources to run the church. But I've seen different ways that people sometimes even force people to give. And you gave a very straightforward example that if you don't give your tithe, you are under a curse ... Sometimes people are

asking everyone who has given: 'Can you stand up for everyone to see you?' sort of thing.

The participant discussed the example of financial giving in a church context. In this context, tithing should be understood as a Christian practice of expecting committed believers to give ten per cent of their pre-tax income to their church. The reference to a curse falling on people for failing to pay their tithes is based on the book of Malachi. In Malachi 3.6–12, God rebukes those who withhold their tithes, stating that they are under a curse. By contrast, those who bring the full tithe into the storehouse will receive abundant blessing from God. The participant's point was that those who understand the biblical background hear the injunction differently from those who have no familiarity with this text. Thus, biblical literacy is an important part of determining whether an action is abusive or problematic.

These discussions of subjectivity served as further reminders of the supreme usefulness of Professor Lisa Oakley's continuum. Not all would agree with everything individual participants have stated; but the point is that sometimes the discussion is all that is needed to raise awareness, challenge inappropriate behaviour and deal with abuse.

Cultural competence

If experiences of abuse are subjective, then the response to perceived abuse must be culturally competent, nimble footed and compassionate, but clear. It must be able to distinguish unhelpful behaviour from abuse. It should be aware of hidden dynamics and alert to unconscious biases.

Based on a difficult situation they had experienced, a participant argued that you need policies, procedures and processes; otherwise, when things go wrong, responses are ad hoc and damaging. When process is not followed, abuse can flourish. But ill-judged process can also cause harm.

Another participant explained:

> I think there should still be some guidelines or framework, or some kind of practice-based approach, but allowing for the flexibility to implement some of these things. For example, you know, the safeguarding policies and procedure that could be across different phase settings. You don't need too much divergence from one to another. But, for example, you know, around training, education, community culture, I think there's scope to do a little bit more of a tailored approach to implement this.

You need policies and procedures, but they must be fit for purpose. As a third participant said, there should be culturally competent education. Those delivering training and education must bear in mind the cultural background and assumptions of those being trained. The specific point concerned Nigerian expectations around discipline in comparison with the norm in the UK. For example, a Nigerian adult man might consider an appropriate way of disciplining a child to be to twist the child's ear, which would be regarded as inappropriate in a UK setting. But the way to deal with it is through training and education, and with an explanation of safeguarding policies and procedures, rather than through involving the authorities. Education should include information on alternative, non-physical discipline and control strategies.

Education should also develop agency. Passivity is a key problem – abuse does not just happen; it results from people looking the other way. One participant suggested:

> This is tricky as well, because I think the issue is that some people who are really undergoing abusive situations may not even recognize that situation as abusive. And so the issue of whether you have the choice of reporting or something like that doesn't even come in.

People's cultural framework may presume that those in authority are to be obeyed or that a particular practice is positive. Simply stating this is wrong will not change anything. A more nuanced approach is required. Another participant said:

Education and awareness and information are going to be really critical. And then, immediately after that, I think agency becomes really important. So, the first thing for me would be identification of the abuse, and then, secondly, what can you then do?

Or, to put it another way:

> I think you harm agency when you abuse. Once a person has been abused and, like we said earlier, they may not even know that that's happened to them. It's only through investigation we find out that what was going on for this period of time was actually abuse. And if they signed up to something, gave something, agreed to something during that period … I think the abused lost their sense of agency.

If we are to develop appropriate responses to spiritual abuse, we must develop agency and education in culturally competent ways. As a participant pointed out, education must be empowering: 'We have to show compassion, and we have to show understanding. We don't have to agree with people, but we need to win their trust.' Education about spiritual abuse must be done carefully:

> I think language is also important. Because this comes down to religion … this could easily be misinterpreted and abused by other people: 'This is wrong. How dare you say this about our practices? Are you pointing the finger at us?' … So, it needs to be done with a degree of impartiality.

Another person stated, 'I think there's something about listening and developing the skills to understand and scrutinize what is going on.' The participant added, 'There's nothing that replaces survivor testimonies.' Yet care must be taken:

> I think the challenge with survivor testimonies is about extrapolating from one person's testimony to something bigger … So, if a survivor is giving a testimony and says, 'Look, this started with walking down the street, with people calling me names,

and then I lost my job. And then I was kicked out of my home' ... The danger is that the starting point – it seemed to be when 'they call me names' – and therefore, if we stop calling people names, these other things won't happen. And of course that's not the case. The name calling is happening because these other structural things are already in place and have been put in place for a long time. Structural discrimination. This rhetoric coming from [a] high level, you know, from our political leaders and this kind of thing.

Two points flow from this discussion. First, we have to proceed with caution. We must be careful in our use of language and in our approach to educating people. There should be no sense of apportioning blame or of attacking others. Second, different ways of teaching are required. While being careful not to cram too much into a session, we should nevertheless plan a variety of culturally appropriate activities and approaches, including (but not limited to) survivor testimony. Chapter 4 deals with these issues through exploring agency and education.

4

The Power of Choice and Learning

> I was terrified – I didn't know what I would say. The bishop was very tall, very big, very purple. He said that physical comfort was the best kind. He said, 'suffer the little children to come unto me'. And then he abused me. (Lord, 2019, p. 99)

The problem with spiritual abuse is that it robs people of power. The more I have thought about it, the more I realize that people need both to understand the problems that spiritual abuse causes and to be able to do something about the problems. They need agency and educating: A&E.

Agency

By 'agency', I mean the ability to respond proactively to the risk and reality of spiritual abuse. Developing agency is a form of empowerment of individuals and groups to recognize their own weaknesses and vulnerabilities, and to recognize the strengths and resources that are necessary for dealing with spiritual abuse. How do we help religious people to make good choices that keep them and their loved ones safe?

I will discuss two areas: first, developing individual agency; and second, cultural change.

Developing individual agency

What should we do in response to the risk of spiritual abuse? Here, I use examples from two authors writing about responding to sexual abuse. First, I explore Catherine Beaumont's suggestions for supporting survivors; second, I look at Marcus Erooga's ideas about equipping bystanders to act if they see something that does not feel right.

Catherine Beaumont discusses how the local church can support adult survivors of child sexual abuse. She suggests that we help people to understand what God's love for them means. She wants the Church to equip survivors of abuse with the agency to respond to their past trauma and act in a way that prevents abuse occurring again.

Throughout her book Beaumont tells stories of how a congregation might develop appropriate responses. The survivor of abuse can always make choices in their own best interest. They have enough agency to take care of themselves.

Beaumont's final example is of a young woman challenging a churchwarden over inappropriate sexual behaviour during the Peace in a church service. This is a striking and powerful example of agency. First, the young woman herself shouts, 'Take your hands off me!', in the middle of the Peace, disrupting the service. Second, the vicar does not overrule the interruption and simply move things on; rather, the vicar pauses the service. He allows the young woman to speak, hears a disclosure from another young woman and ensures appropriate action is taken swiftly. Third, the church council and diocesan authorities also take swift, appropriate action. This is the ideal: everybody reacts appropriately to disclosure because they know it is more important to keep people safe than to simply go on with what they were doing (Beaumont, 2020, pp. 128–9).

Marcus Erooga discusses the potential that 'bystander programmes' have for developing individual agency, enabling people to resist being groomed by abusers and supporting those at risk of significant harm. Erooga outlines four key areas of learning.

1 Policies and procedures, especially a code of conduct, should be in place and implemented consistently, every time, with no exceptions. This enables those with little or no power in the organization to challenge those with status who behave inappropriately. The aim of regular training in safeguarding policy and procedures is to empower junior staff to provide

a description of behaviour in neutral language, which simply notes that the code of conduct has not been followed. For example: 'The minister was alone in a bedroom with a teenage boy.'
2 Monitoring behaviours is the aim, rather than judging people. Staff and volunteers need to be trained on the specific behaviours to look for and given the agency to ask questions about problematic behaviour. Those of low status thus have agency; they simply report the behaviour they have witnessed: 'I saw him stroking the intern's hair. She looked unhappy.'
3 Everyone, every bystander, has a critical role to play in prevention. Everyone must be involved in ensuring the policies, procedures and the code of conduct are enforced and followed. If there is no opportunity to abuse, then abuse cannot take place.
4 The media also have an important role to play in helping people better understand and accurately frame sexual abuse. Those reporting on abuse must be careful and precise in giving details, providing context and talking to experts. This applies just as much to spiritual as to sexual abuse. (Erooga, 2018, pp. 170–81)

Cultural change

In this section, I will introduce child sexual abuse in the Catholic Church as an example of an unhealthy culture. I then give two examples of how to change culture: ESSTA (empowerment, supervision, support, training and awareness) and organizational values as prompts for leadership teams to develop healthy cultures.

In her study of child sexual abuse in the Catholic Church, Marie Keenan reflects upon power and powerlessness. Her research includes detailed interviews with priests who abused children. Through these conversations, she identified a contradiction in the culture of the Catholic Church. Priests were simultaneously put on a pedestal ('Father knows best') and, at the same time, they had no real power or choices about where they lived and what they were expected to do. Spiritually, they were the elite. Socially, sexually and relationally, they were completely immature. These priests were people of power who were simultaneously powerless.

Keenan argues that the Catholic theological understanding of ontological change that occurs at ordination to the priesthood set these men up to assume themselves to be superior, and hence powerful. At the same time, however, it trapped them in expectations of behaviour and separation that rendered them powerless to deal with their own sexual desires: desires that, unfortunately for some, found expression in abusive behaviour. Priests were respected leaders, representatives of Christ on Earth, whose word was law, yet they had the emotional maturity of teenagers just coming to terms with puberty.

Marie Keenan explains that the Catholic clergy she interviewed lacked personal awareness, real and honest dialogue with others, and reflective space. They were trained to be obedient rather than have agency. They were emotionally isolated and lonely people, lacking the tools to develop honest relationships; so they developed all kinds of inappropriate coping mechanisms, including alcoholism and inappropriate sexual activity. Keenan argues that these men were not paedophiles. They were trapped by a model of 'Perfect Celibate Clerical Masculinity': a model that they failed to live up to. They needed to develop the agency, self-understanding and vocation as priests that were more realistic for who they were as human beings. Such changes can occur only if there is a significant cultural and organizational shift (Keenan, 2012, pp. 235–48).

Safeguarding is not primarily an issue of policy, but one of organizational culture. Indeed, the single most important practical steps any religious group can take to become safer is to develop a healthier culture.

I used to be the chair of governors of a primary school; I can vividly remember a conversation I had with the head teacher about one of his staff. She had not responded appropriately to a safeguarding disclosure. It was not because she had not attended training: she had been present at the mandatory annual refresher every year she had worked in the school. It was because safeguarding was not part of her world-view, her culture. Places of worship and faith communities face the same cultural challenge. We often defer unnecessarily quickly to the spiritual authority of a single leader; those leaders do not always have the maturity or objectivity to recognize the potential for spiritual abuse in the setting over which they have authority.

What do we mean when we talk about a safe organizational culture? What does a healthy culture look like? It will be one where there are appropriate policies and procedures in place to ensure that everyone knows how to keep themselves and others safe. It will be an organization in which everyone is held accountable, especially those in senior leadership positions. It will be an organization where inappropriate behaviour is questioned and challenged, regardless of who the perpetrator of the behaviour is.

One way to create a healthy culture is to foster an approach focused on empowerment, supervision, support, training and awareness: ESSTA (Oakley and Humphreys, 2019, pp. 134–5).

Empowerment: There is a tension, here, between recognizing and accepting the authority of those who are spiritual teachers and, at the same time, challenging their behaviour when it is inappropriate. The purpose of empowering a religious community is not to destroy the ability of leaders to teach their congregations or to pass on the faith. Rather, it is to provide a safety valve: a way of stopping a spiritual teacher stepping beyond their authority. In a healthy culture, matters of faith and doctrine can be discussed and debated. The wisdom of those who have spent decades studying and developing themselves should be recognized, but it is not to be given undue weight or allowed to mask abuse.

Supervision: Being a religious leader can be a lonely experience. There may be no one to confide in or seek advice from. This may be one of the reasons why religious leaders make mistakes and overstep the boundaries of their authority. It is better for everyone if religious leaders are given time and space to reflect on their decisions, as well as a safe space to explore what they can learn from their mistakes. This may involve peer-to-peer engagement; alternatively, it may involve a designated supervisor. There could be financial costs associated with supervision, in travelling or in paying the supervisor. Congregations should not see this as a frivolous luxury but as a necessary expenditure to keep their leader – and themselves – spiritually healthy.

Support: Spiritual abuse is a complex phenomenon and will be experienced differently by different people. At a very basic level, congregation members can offer personal support to a victim of spiritual abuse. But they must be guided by the person who needs support, rather than presuming that they know best. Different people will need different types of support; and the type of support an individual may want will vary from day to day. The most crucial aspect of support is to be open and non-judgemental. We are to respond to what we are asked to do, rather than decide what is best for someone else.

Training: The purpose of safeguarding training is primarily to embed safeguarding within the organization's culture. It is easy for these issues to slip to the back of the mind; so regular refreshers and update sessions are helpful for bringing them back to the forefront of everyone's thinking. Honest and open discussions, a periodic audit, and a willingness to recognize and deal with mistakes will all flow from regular training and attention to the importance of safeguarding.

Awareness: Crucially, we must recognize that spiritual abuse could happen in our context. We must even recognize that we could – perhaps unintentionally – engage in abusive behaviour. In my experience, using scenarios to plan for a crisis and the reality of responding to a crisis are two very different things. But without engaging in scenario-planning, without thinking through what a good response might be, we are unlikely to develop the skills to respond quickly in a crisis. Being aware that some unspecified thing might go wrong helps us to respond well when the crisis hits.

All this is primarily the responsibility of those in leadership.

A second way for leaders to bring about the needed cultural change is to focus on six aspects of organizational culture and values (Oakley and Humphreys, 2019, pp. 133–51, based on the work of Johnson, Scholes and Whittington, 2008).

First, ritual and routines: do the everyday activities and behaviours that are acceptable within the faith-based organization model foster safer practice and the importance of healthy attitudes and beliefs for all? While experience is important, it must not stand in the way of imagining different, safer, smarter, healthier ways of leading and running an organization.

Second, control systems: does the way the faith-based organization is controlled and governed ensure a healthy culture is monitored with as much care as strategy, mission and vision? This is not to argue that leaders should not lead but, rather, that there must be space for discussion and challenge. Coercive control restricts or removes freedom to challenge and disagree. A healthy culture invites, respects and learns from challenge and questions, welcoming disagreement when it is appropriate and necessary.

Third, organizational structures: how are people valued within the formal structures, reporting lines and accountability systems? How are unofficial, unspoken rules challenged, deconstructed and monitored to prevent the development of unhealthy subcultures? Oakley and Humphreys are not interested in dictating the type of structure a faith-based organization employs; rather, they are concerned that the nature of the structure is understood by all and that it models a safe, healthy culture.

Fourth, stories and commentary: how are past events and experiences, when unhealthy or abusive behaviour was disclosed, talked about and referred to? Oakley and Humphreys are clear that we need to talk about spiritual abuse: not only the stories of failures to deal with the problem, but also accounts of good practice, which serve as a model for others.

Fifth, symbolism and messaging, which refers to the visual identity of the faith-based organization and the message its identity conveys in relation to its values, culture, mission and vision. Is it obvious that the faith-based organization takes safeguarding seriously? For example, is there a safeguarding commitment statement visible to everyone? Is it easy to find out whom to contact if you have a safeguarding concern? Does what the faith-based organization say it does match up with what it actually does?

Sixth, power dynamics: where is formal and informal power located? What role do leaders have in decision-making? How empowering and inclusive is the faith-based organization's environment? Are leaders held appropriately accountable? Are they able to be suitably vulnerable? Are they supported to develop and grow? Is diversity valued and supported?

Making good choices

People can make good choices if they feel safe and have the support and space to think through the consequences of what they are about to do. I have introduced two ways of developing individual agency: supporting survivors and equipping bystanders to speak out about abuse. I have also discussed three aspects of organizational culture. I introduced an example of an unhealthy culture and made two suggestions for how to keep a culture healthy. This may feel overwhelming. But there is no expectation that you do everything at once. Responding to spiritual abuse is a long process: it's a marathon, not a sprint. Decide on which one thing you should do next and begin working on that. If it seems too difficult right now, read on for ideas about how to learn more about responding to spiritual abuse.

Education

The strapline for the organization I lead, the St Philip's Centre, is 'Learning to live well together'. We talk about 'learning' rather than 'studying' because our focus is on informal education from which you learn life skills. Just as you can learn to ride a bike, knit or bake cakes, you can learn how to respond to spiritual abuse. Of course, some people need to study the issue in detail. But for most of us, learning is enough. But what is the most effective method of helping people to learn about the risks and impact of spiritual abuse? In this section, I will reflect on two points. First,

I will look at learning from past mistakes and, second, at what engaging education looks like. We all need to keep learning how to respond to spiritual abuse.

Learning from the past

Mistakes are repeated all too often, especially if we do not take the time to learn from our own, and others', mistakes. The Methodist Church has identified ten things to learn from their review of past safeguarding cases (Methodist Church, 2016).

1 Abuse and risk are not always recognized.
2 There is a huge and ongoing impact of abuse on those who have been harmed.
3 Abuse that has occurred in a church setting is deeply distressing and is a devastating breach of trust.
4 There is a need for a greater development of listening skills.
5 People in the Church are still not responding well to serious situations.
6 People find it difficult to recognize that those who are their colleagues and friends – and have done good things – can also do harm.
7 Responding well to the church congregation in difficult safeguarding situations continues to be a challenge.
8 Recording practice has improved but record keeping is still not consistent enough.
9 Effective working with other agencies still requires development.
10 There has been, and remains, insufficient understanding of the significance of safeguarding concerns among those who hold leadership roles in the Methodist Church.

The document that summarizes the themes was written as a guide for developing further training in safeguarding for Methodist Christians. This reminds us of the importance of education as a key theme in responding to spiritual abuse. At least four of the themes also emphasize the importance of developing agency, which reminds us how interlinked agency and education are.

1 Good listeners have a strong sense of their own agency and power. By listening well, they can unlock problems and begin to develop solutions. They are ready and able to act.
2 For people in the Church to respond well to abuse, they must be empowered and equipped to make difficult judgement calls in complex situations.
3 This is especially true of ministers dealing with allegations of abuse within their own congregations. Those who abuse may well have groomed the entire congregation; so the situation of a whistleblower, even if that person is the minister, can be a lonely and painful one. A strong sense of personal responsibility and strongly developed individual agency are fundamental requirements for successfully challenging misconceptions and enabling open discussion of the possibility of abuse.
4 Working with external authorities requires individuals to have their own ability to act. It is not enough to think you must talk to the police, social services or other groups. You must have the confidence and ability to do so, including the courage to challenge inadequate responses by those agencies.

Engaging education

We should also think about what engaging learning looks like. Spiritual abuse is a scary topic. It can be tough to talk about. A boring PowerPoint or hour-long monologue from a trainer will not help anyone to learn anything. How can we do better? Parker Palmer and Frances Ward have some great ideas for how learning can be dynamic and active.

Palmer: The Courage to Teach

In *The Courage to Teach*, Parker Palmer argues that good teaching comes from the heart and so requires excellent self-knowledge: 'As I teach, I project the condition of my soul onto my students, my subject, and our way of being together' (Palmer, 1998, p. 3). Those wishing to educate others on the topic of spiritual abuse must first engage in serious self-reflection as to their own use of power. Teachers stand at the intersection of the public and the personal. They must teach what they care about; but, because they care, their teaching cannot remain dispassionate and theoretical. Yet at the same time, teaching motivated by fear is the worst possible kind. But fear is all around teaching and classrooms, teachers and students. This interplay of passion and fear resonates with education on safeguarding and the risks of abuse. Those who campaign for greater awareness of the risk of spiritual abuse do so with passion and a deep concern for the well-being of their fellow humans. Religious institutions are fearful of being caught out, fearful of the consequences of past failures, and fearful of what those they engage with might reveal of their own experiences or inadequate understanding. Such strong emotions must be acknowledged at the start of any learning process. Palmer suggests that rather than being either teacher- or student-centred, learning should in fact be subject-centred. The focus is on finding the truth together, which eliminates the power dynamic, and so frees us from fear, posturing and protecting ourselves; instead, it enables us to teach and learn together.

Parker Palmer argues that six elements are necessary to create a safe space for teaching and learning.

1. The space should be bounded and open. Boundaries provide focus; openness allows the subject to be explored and discoveries made.
2. The space should be hospitable and 'charged'. Hospitality implies a space that is inviting, safe and trustworthy: a place where people want to learn. But there must also be a charge; for if students are 'to learn at the deepest levels they must not feel so safe that they fall asleep: they need to feel the risks inherent in pursuing the deep things of the world or of the soul' (Palmer, 1998, p. 75).
3. The space should invite the voice of the individual and the voice of the group. Both individuals and the collective must be able to express themselves appropriately.
4. The space should honour the 'little' stories of the students and the 'big' stories of the disciplines and tradition. Personal stories must be told; but they cannot be the only point of refer-

ence or 'we easily become lost in narcissism' (Palmer, 1998, p. 76). The 'big' stories, those of universal relevance, must also be told. All stories must be given equal respect.
5 The space should support solitude and surround it with the resources of community. Students need time for individual reflection; the integrity of the students' inner life must be respected. Learning also demands community and discussion as our ignorance is aired, our ideas are tested and our biases challenged. An authentic learning community balances individual and group time.
6 The space should welcome both silence and speech. We do not need to speak all the time; people learn in silence as well as through listening and talking. (Palmer, 1998, pp. 74–7)

How can these six elements be deployed in teaching about spiritual abuse? We should be clear what we are – and are not – talking about. We begin by defining what spiritual abuse is. We must make clear the real-world impact of spiritual abuse through the authentic voices of those who have experienced, and have had to respond to, the realities of spiritual abuse. This requires the voices and actions of individuals and of institutions to be heard. Any training should have time for quiet, individual reflection, group work and plenary sessions. There should be opportunity for discussion and debate, for disagreement and learning. Any learning should be engaging and challenging: the participants should leave the session changed in some way.

Ward: Full of Character

In *Full of Character*, Frances Ward explains that she is wondering 'what education is *for* in today's highly complex and rather scary world' (Ward, 2019, p. 28). She has a lot to say. I will focus on her nine essays on the character of a teacher.

1 Thankfulness: in an educational context, thankfulness allows those being educated to receive learning as a gift to be enjoyed, nourished and carried on throughout life.
2 Self-forgetfulness, which means not worrying about who I am

but focusing, instead, on learning new skills, and being humble enough to be a student who does not know the answers.
3. Carefulness: Ward's focus here is on early years, particularly the importance of babies learning to attach properly to those who care for them. A care-filled introduction to the world will enable babies to grow up into children and then adults who flourish.
4. Playfulness, which Ward regards as essential to human flourishing. It is through play that we understand the boundaries of the world, our place in it and the way we interact with others. It is through play that we can explore our fears, uncertainties and what we do not know. Even worship can be a form of play, as we set aside the need to be functional and purposeful and instead engage with the profound mystery who God is.
5. Resourcefulness, which is more than resilience and more than a reactive ability to cope. It is about responding to challenges and turning things around for the benefit of others. Resourceful people enable themselves and others to flourish, even in adversity. Ward discusses Angela Duckworth's *Grit*, noting the importance of continually doing challenging things to grow as a human being.
6. Thoughtfulness, thinking deeply and recognizing complexity: we resist the impulse to give in to a simplistic view of the world as one of black-and-white opposites. Instead, we give deep, focused attention to what is going on.
7. Fruitfulness, especially the human need to work: we must not be only task oriented; we should not merely focus on productivity, in the sense of producing more widgets per hour. Rather, we must develop a fruitful life, which fosters creativity, promotes satisfaction through interaction with others, includes a sense of adventure and cultivates the imagination.
8. Truthfulness: truth is not a possession; it is to be sought. Truth must be spoken to those in power; it is characterized by accuracy and simplicity. It requires the development of critical thinking skills and the courage to speak out.
9. Hopefulness: 'Hope is not easy optimism, but a deep wisdom that recognises the promise implicit in all things, situations and people' (Ward, 2019, p. 226). Returning to Angela Duck-

worth's writing on *Grit*, Ward suggests reflecting on how the work we have done has made a positive contribution to society. She asks us to think about small but meaningful ways current work can be enhanced through connection to core values and to find inspiration in a purposeful role model. Hope is not mere optimism. It can face even the darkest experience of despair 'because it looks to a future that holds out the promise of fullness of life'. (Ward, 2019, p. 237)

Imagine education on the risks and impact of spiritual abuse shaped by these characteristics: being thankful for the good that exists in life, even in the darkest of circumstances; forgetting your own agenda or fears, and seeking primarily the good of others; fostering a care-filled, nurturing approach to tackling complex and painful topics; and yet, at the same time, encouraging a willingness to experiment and explore, and to ask, 'What if?' Imagine standing in difficulty, but also envisaging a brighter future where learning is resourceful and seeks the flourishing of all who are engaged in dealing with the grim reality of spiritual abuse. Think of a process in which we recognize the complexity of the situation and are not defined by simple pseudo-explanations; one where we see teaching on spiritual abuse as a path to fruitfulness and flourishing, speaking the truth of what has happened, regardless of the cost. All of this is shaped primarily by hope: hope that people can learn and change and that a brighter future is possible.

Teaching and learning require courage, creativity and a willingness to take risks. It is tempting for organizations to ignore the problems or numb people into compliance via PowerPoint. But that will not help anyone learn anything useful. Building on the suggestions above, there is potential for creative exercises, for using video and audio materials, and for multisensory approaches that encourage people to move around the learning space. There is advice in subsequent chapters for how to put these ideas into practice, to help people learn how to respond to spiritual abuse.

PART III

Lessons

In Chapter 5, I discuss six high-profile cases of spiritual abuse in Church of England settings. Each case tells a story of lost trust, broken leadership, and the power dynamics that allowed abuse to happen. I look at what went wrong and how lessons from these cases can guide future work to prevent spiritual abuse.

In Chapter 6, I reflect on what the Bible says about leadership and the abuse of power. From warnings in the Hebrew Scriptures, to Jesus' rebuke of corrupt leaders and Paul's concerns about control in the early Church, I explore how these ancient texts speak directly to the modern problem of spiritual abuse.

5

Spiritual Abuse in the Church of England

The Church of England is in crisis, and will only redeem the astonishing mess that it has made of its response to all this by full, honest and transparent ownership of that crisis. Ownership will come about through the speaking of truth to power. (Fife and Gilo, 2019, p. xi).

Discussion of spiritual abuse can be very emotional and challenging at times. The tone adopted is crucial for ensuring open and productive engagement. Any sense of finger pointing, singling out a particular community for rebuke or blame would be entirely counterproductive. This is why in public workshops, when I discuss specific examples of spiritual abuse, I focus on publicly documented Church of England cases. First, I do so because I am a Church of England vicar and therefore I'm criticizing my own denomination, rather than attacking others. Second, I do so because these are cases that are on public record. In this way, I avoid accidentally sharing privileged or confidential information. Because of this focus, this chapter is probably of greatest use for Anglicans. But as with the Jewish cases discussed in Chapter 1, the lessons are applicable to most, if not all, religious and spiritual contexts.

This chapter was one of the hardest to write, both because of the terrible subject matter and because of the steady stream of reports and disclosures. Doubtless more will have come to light between finishing this draft in early March 2025 and publication.

I have selected six case studies to discuss. Rather than examine each case in turn I will instead use the cases to test my theory of agency and education. The chapter is divided into five parts.

First, I give a brief outline of each case, in alphabetical order by surname. Second, I reflect on agency. Third, I lay out the lessons learned about education. Fourth, I highlight the connections with the conversations included in my research. Fifth, I draw conclusions.

Overview of the six cases

The cases I discuss are those relating to Peter Ball, Timothy Davis, Jonathan Fletcher, Michael Hall, Mike Pilavachi and John Smyth. Information on all six cases is readily available; between them, they cover a range of traditions within the Church of England.

Peter Ball

The primary source of information on Peter Ball is the report into the Anglican Church conducted by the Independent Inquiry into Child Sexual Abuse (IICSA). The report explains that

> Peter Ball was ordained in 1957. With his brother he founded a monastic order, the Community of the Glorious Ascension, of which he was a leading member for 20 years. In 1977, he became the Suffragan Bishop of Lewes in the Diocese of Chichester. He became the Diocesan Bishop of Gloucester in 1992, a post he held for less than two years. In 2015 he was convicted of two offences of indecent assault and an offence of misconduct in a public office, which involved 16 different victims. By his plea he accepted that he 'obtained sexual gratification from the deliberate manipulation of vulnerable young men'. (IICSA, 2019, p. 110)

The IICSA heard allegations against Peter Ball from 33 individuals, ranging as far back as 1969, when he was the Prior of the Community of the Glorious Ascension. While Ball was the Bishop of Lewes, young men would live with him in his diocesan home. He groomed, exploited and committed offences against them.

Despite his own diocesan bishop being aware of this behaviour, Peter Ball was appointed as the Bishop of Gloucester.

In 1992, Neil Todd, a young man who was living with Ball, attempted suicide. Todd subsequently tried to raise the alarm within the Church; he reported allegations against Peter Ball to clergy, including two bishops. After his second suicide attempt, Neil Todd's parents reported his allegations to the police.

> An investigation by Gloucestershire Constabulary identified a further six complainants. Lambeth Palace received letters containing accounts of sexual misconduct from seven teenagers and young men. In 1993, despite there being four potential charges available relating to offences concerning three young men, Peter Ball received a caution for one single offence of gross indecency with Neil Todd. As a result, he resigned as the Bishop of Gloucester on 7 March 1993. (IICSA, 2019, p. 110)

This case has been widely publicized; a two-part documentary film of the case is used in Church of England safeguarding training.

Timothy Davis

Timothy Davis was the Vicar of Christ Church, Abingdon. He was subject to a complaint under the Clergy Discipline Measure (CDM) 2003, brought by the Archdeacon of Dorchester, Judith French. Information about this case is found in the tribunal paperwork (Church of England, 2017) and the subsequent lessons-learned review, carried out by Lamb and Briden (2020). The charge under the CDM 2003 was that

> the Participant Timothy Davis was between January 2012 and September 2013 guilty of conduct unbecoming or inappropriate to the office and work of a clerk in Holy Orders through the abuse of spiritual power and authority over W1 then a person aged 15–16 in that:
>
> 1 Throughout the said period being engaged in a mentoring so intense that W1 was put under unacceptable pressure hav-

ing regard to his age and maturity and was deprived of his freedom of choice as to whether to continue with the same
2. On occasions too numerous to particularise during the said period was in breach of the safeguarding requirements by being alone with W1 whether in his house or in the vicarage or other places and on occasions deliberately touching him albeit not in a sexual manner
3. Under the guise of his authority sought to control by the use of admonition, Scripture, prayer and revealed prophecy the life of W1 and/or his relationship with his girlfriend
4. Under the guise of his authority procured and retained the consent of W1's parents to this relationship.
5. Throughout the said period failed to have any regard to the propriety of the said conduct and/or its effect on others and in particular on W1. (Church of England, 2017, pp. 1–2)

The tribunal decided that all five charges detailed above were true, and that Davis was therefore 'guilty of misconduct which was unbecoming and inappropriate to the work and office of a clerk in Holy Orders' (Church of England, 2017, p. 18).

Jonathan Fletcher

Jonathan Fletcher (JF) was the Vicar of Emmanuel Church, Wimbledon (ECW), from 1982 to 2012. ECW is a proprietary chapel (that is, founded by an individual) and therefore acted largely independently of the Anglican diocese of Southwark, where it is located. The primary source of information on Fletcher is the review conducted by the safeguarding charity thirtyone:eight (thirtyone:eight, 2021). thirtyone:eight was commissioned by ECW in 2019 to undertake an independent, lessons-learned review in response to the growing concerns and allegations made in relation to Jonathan Fletcher. The two reviewers, Professor Lisa Oakley and Mr Simon Plant, were overseen by an independent advisory board. Information was provided to the review by 98 participants; 59 were members or former members of ECW; 33 were role holders or former role holders. The number of people who experienced the behaviours described in the review was 27, some of whom self-identified as victims; others stated the behaviour was consensual, not abusive, and did not identify as victims. The review does not indicate how many people were in either group. Jonathan Fletcher was invited to participate but did not do so. Due to restrictions resulting from the Covid-19 pandemic, all participation was remote (by phone, email, video call or letter) (thirtyone:eight, 2021, pp. 4–5).

The harmful forms of behaviour reported included coercion and control, bullying, naked massages and saunas, forfeits (including spanking with a gym shoe) and ice baths. One serious incident of a sexual nature was also reported: 'One participant reported that JF told him to perform a sex act in front of him and when he did not, JF performed the act instead.' In the view of the reviewers, this constituted a 'gross abuse of power'.

At the time of publication of the review, Jonathan Fletcher had not been charged with or found guilty of any offence (thirtyone:eight, 2021, p. 5). He was, however, charged on 10 July 2024 for offences dating between 1973 and 1999, including eight counts of indecent assault and one of grievous bodily harm. On 12 August 2024, Jonathan Fletcher appeared at Kingston Crown Court charged with eight counts of indecent assault on a man aged 16 or over and one further count of Section 18 grievous bodily harm, with intent. He pleaded 'not guilty' to these alleged crimes. The case was referred for trial on Monday, 30 June 2025.

Michael Hall

Michael Hall was the Priest in Charge, and then Vicar, of St Margaret's Church, Tylers Green, in Buckinghamshire from 1981 to 2000. The information on this case comes from a lessons-learned review conducted by Elaine and Patrick Hopkinson in 2023. The Diocese of Oxford commissioned the review after the tragic suicide of a young man who had been a member of St Margaret's congregation when Hall was the vicar. In the days before his death, this young man spoke to a member of the clergy about being unable to move on from the depression and trauma caused by Michael Hall. The current vicar raised concerns with the diocesan safeguarding team who commissioned a thorough, independent investigation.

> The investigation concluded on the balance of probabilities that Reverend Hall had spiritually abused a significant number of the congregation, and that he had engaged in sexually inappropriate behaviour with members of the congregation, which was witnessed by children and young people ... Reverend Hall is described as a bully, who used coercion and control to silence dissent, isolate the congregation, make them dependent on him and to exploit them. He emotionally abused people and used scripture and fear of hell to control them. (Hopkinson and Hopkinson, 2023, p. 3)

Michael Hall died in June 2021.

Mike Pilavachi

Mike Pilavachi co-founded Soul Survivor Church, Watford, with Matt Redman in 1993. This charismatic evangelical church also ran an annual youth festival that regularly saw thousands of young people make commitments to follow Jesus. Pilavachi was widely regarded as a gifted and effective evangelist, whose ministry had an impact on tens if not hundreds of thousands of young people. In April 2023, he was subject to a safeguarding complaint and stepped back from ministry while it was investigated. Below is the Church of England statement on the conclusion of that investigation:

> The internal Church investigation into Mike Pilavachi, being conducted by the National Safeguarding Team, NST, and the diocese of St Albans, has now concluded. Having explored the safeguarding concerns fully, according to House of Bishops guidance, the investigation team has concluded that they are substantiated. These relate to conduct in his leadership and ministry, both before and after he was ordained in 2012, spanning 40 years from his time as a youth leader through to the current day.

The overall substantiated concerns are described as an abuse of power relating to his ministry, and spiritual abuse; described in guidance as 'a form of emotional and psychological abuse characterised by a systematic pattern of coercive and controlling behaviour in a religious context'. It was concluded that he used his spiritual authority to control people and that his coercive and controlling behaviour led to inappropriate relationships, the physical wrestling of youths and massaging of young male interns. (Church of England, 2023)

In April 2024, a short documentary film, *Let There Be Light*, was released giving further insights into the concerns expressed about Pilavachi's behaviour. In September 2024, a review into the case was published (Scolding and Fullbrook, 2024). It set out six concerns:

1 Pilavachi developed inappropriately close relationships with young men, and women, followed by long periods of 'ghosting': breaking off all contact with an individual for no apparent reason. This was confusing and hurtful for those concerned and led to long-term psychological damage for some.
2 Pilavachi promised roles within the Soul Survivor organizations that did not always materialize. He raised the expectations of young people unnecessarily before abandoning them after a period of two or three years.
3 Pilavachi was inappropriately controlling in the way he ran Soul Survivor Church and the summer festivals.
4 Pilavachi engaged in lengthy, one-to-one wrestling sessions in private with young men in the 1990s, 2000s and possibly even the 2010s. The young people did not want to do this and felt uncomfortable about it.
5 Pilavachi gave one-to-one massages to young men in private in the 2000s. The men were semi-naked (sometimes only in their underwear) and would lie on Pilavachi's bed. The young people did not ask for massages; many felt deeply ashamed after them. Two men claimed the activity fulfilled a sexual outlet for Pilavachi. He disputes this.

6 Pilavachi, and others, displayed poor safeguarding practice in several cases involving third parties. (Scolding and Fullbrook 2024, pp. 5–6)

A further review was published in 2025; it examined the relationship between New Wine and Soul Survivor, including what level of responsibility New Wine bore in relation to Pilavachi (Scolding, Henderson and Fullbrook, 2025).

John Smyth

John Smyth was

> a serious and prolific abuser of boys and young men, both in the UK and in Africa. Tragically for his victims, he was never bought to justice for the abuse; he died in August 2018, in Cape Town, South Africa, at the age of 75, while under investigation by Hampshire Police. (Makin, 2024, p. 8. I have primarily used the Makin Review. Graystone, 2021, also covers the case in detail.)

The sheer scale of the abuse perpetrated by Smyth is staggering. A report produced in 1982, known as the Ruston Report is cited in the Makin Review:

> The scale and severity of the practice was horrific. Five of the 13 I have seen were in it only for a short time. Between them they had 12 beatings and about 650 strokes. The other 8 received about 14,000 strokes: 2 of them having some 8,000 strokes over the three years. The others were involved for one year or 18 months. 8 spoke of bleeding on most occasions ('I could feel the blood splattering on my legs', 'I was bleeding for 3½ weeks', 'I fainted sometime after a severe beating'). I have seen bruised and scored buttocks, some two-and-a-half months after the beating. Beatings of 100 strokes for masturbation, 400 for pride, and one of 800 strokes for some undisclosed 'fall' are recorded. (Makin, 2024, p. 17)

The Makin Review adds:

> Evidence considered in this Review suggests that 16 Winchester College students were physically abused, with a further six to eight who were groomed. A further nine victims were abused who had attended eight other public schools prior to the abuse occurring – we strongly suspect that the true figure is probably greater, hence the probable total of victims from this period being in the order of 26 to 30 victims who were abused by John Smyth in the UK. Of these, at least five were recruited by John Smyth directly from universities, with no pre-existing connection to, or attendance, at Iwerne camps. Approximately 60% of those known to have been abused went to Cambridge University, with the rest attending six other universities. John Smyth actively travelled to and recruited at these universities, mainly via the Christian Unions there, being invited to talk.
>
> There is evidence of John Smyth perpetrating abuse against boys and young men in Zimbabwe, detailed later in this report, with evidence primarily given from an independent investigation carried out there in 1993, known as the Coltart Report. The nature and extent of this is truly shocking and relevant to the learning for this Review. We have been passed detailed statements from people who were aware of this abuse and attempting to prevent it at the time, as well as contemporaneous papers, and from research carried out by one of the UK victims. The number of victims in Africa is estimated at around 85 to 100 male children aged 13 to 17. (Makin, 2024, p. 20)

The Makin Review provides a detailed discussion of the abuse, the institutional cover-up that followed, and the inadequate response of the Church of England. The subsequent events and ongoing (at the time of writing) calls for senior leaders to resign are not discussed.

Agency

Having read about these six cases, I think they show us at least six ways in which people lost their personal agency in the context of spiritual abuse. These are

1. inadvertent or process-driven loss
2. fear-based loss
3. loss due to coercive control
4. loss due to the perceived successful ministry of the perpetrator
5. loss due to the positive behaviours of the perpetrator
6. loss due to the assumption of a quasi-divine position.

Inadvertent or process-driven loss

First, inadvertent or process-driven loss is where the process of investigating an allegation deprives people of agency. The Makin Review took years to be completed; victims felt they were ignored or sidelined.

The clearest example of this type of loss occurred in the Timothy Davis case. As Lamb and Briden explain, two individuals, referred to as W2 (the mother of the victim) and C1 (a clergy person) had meetings with the Bishop of Dorchester, Colin Fletcher, to discuss Davis's behaviour. They came away from these meetings 'under the impression that, through expressing their serious concerns to Bishop Colin, they had made formal complaints against the Reverend Davis which would have initiated a disciplinary process'. They were mistaken in this belief, however, because for a complaint to be acted upon it must be made in writing and accompanied by 'written particulars of the alleged misconduct, together with supporting evidence'. This misunderstanding had a significant impact, particularly in delaying proceedings (Lamb and Briden, 2020, p. 3).

In the end, it was the Archdeacon of Dorchester, Judith French, who brought the complaint under the CDM, following a request from Bishop Colin. He began his request with this comment: 'None of the complainants has asked if they can register a formal complaint under the CDM process' (Lamb and Briden, 2020,

p. 5). This meant that those most affected, notably W1 and W2, lost the right to be informed of, or involved in, all aspects of the case.

The processing of the complaint took much longer than it could have. In addition, while the archdeacon was present at the whole of the tribunal hearing, the witnesses were not. The impact of this inadvertent loss of agency was severe: 'W2 was emphatic that she had felt in the end more damaged by the process of the investigation and of the tribunal than by the original bullying and manipulation' by Timothy Davis (Lamb and Briden, 2020, pp. 4–5).

Recognizing this reality is not the same as blaming anyone. Neither Bishop Colin nor Archdeacon Judith (or, for that matter, anyone else) intended to remove the agency of those who had experienced or witnessed abuse. Rather, it was an inadvertent oversight. Lamb and Briden argue that the problem was more about a lack of process than an individual failing. The initial meetings were not the appropriate place to explain the process of the CDM; but no further opportunity was created, no relevant information was shared with those who brought the complaint, and only minimal support was offered to them. The legal restrictions of the CDM process took agency from those who experienced spiritual abuse. Although W2 and others raised concerns about the lack of communication from Archdeacon Judith, the latter had sound reasons for not being forthcoming, as the reviewers explain:

> Failure to observe the necessary confidentiality of legal proceedings carries serious risks. One is that the evidence of witnesses might be contaminated by information derived from extraneous sources, thereby undermining their credibility. Another is that widespread discussion within a parish, and the adoption of opposing positions, enables a participant to be portrayed as the innocent victim of a faction. Disturbing as it may have seemed at the time, there was good reason for the Archdeacon's reticence. (Lamb and Briden, 2020, p. 7)

If perpetrators of spiritual abuse are to be held legally accountable for their actions, there is potential for the inadvertent loss of agency because of the importance of following legal protocols. This risk could be reduced through education, including by sharing appropriate resources. Lamb and Briden suggest that a short handout could be prepared and made available to all senior clergy, who can then give it to anybody who brings a complaint. This, together with informal education about CDM processes and ways of responding to spiritual abuse, would deal with the risk of inadvertently depriving victims of agency.

Fear-based loss

Second, fear-based loss of agency is a common theme in all the cases. One type of fear was that of the impact on career prospects by refusing to do what the perpetrator demanded. For example, the Fletcher Review found

> that JF was a man of great charisma and of significant influence in this sphere. His ability to exercise this influence came in part from being a deeply influential person within a much broader interconnected network, exercising great influence over career placements and being referred to as a 'king maker'. JF's approval was prized and noted by many as essential for career progression in this constituency. (thirtyone:eight, 2021, p. 6)

Those who wished to have a preaching and teaching career within the conservative evangelical tradition in the Church of England needed Fletcher's approval. Fear of upsetting him meant many complied with behaviours and activities they were otherwise uncomfortable with.

John Smyth is described as follows:

> I will say that he is an unbelievably persuasive man, he was … If you sat in the room with him, you pretty much believed whatever he said.
>
> He was completely unable to accept that he wasn't right, so everything was fine until there was a confrontation or a

disagreement about something, and then if that person just wouldn't agree, then they went separate ways, basically and often very unpleasantly after quite a few arguments and stuff. He did never seem to be able to work something through with someone and just agree to disagree. (Makin, 2024, p. 24)

Thus, people were afraid of Smyth and let him do whatever he wanted. Similarly, the IICSA review into the Peter Ball case explains how individuals were forced to comply with abusive behaviours in order to progress in their careers. For example:

On 21 September 1992, Mr Todd told Peter Ball he intended to go to Crawley Down, a monastery in Sussex, to continue his training. He told police that the night before he left, Peter Ball said they should 'share their love'. Mr Todd said that Peter Ball came to his bedroom that night. They embraced naked. Mr Todd said he felt uncomfortable, embarrassed and ashamed but felt that he had to accede to the request. Obedience, he had been told by Peter Ball, was a fundamental feature of the monastic life. (IICSA, 2019, p. 123)

Peter Ball used his position as a bishop and prior to force vulnerable young men to comply with his abuse, using the fear of a negative impact on their careers to enforce compliance.

A victim in the Pilavachi case said:

I lived in a constant state of needing Mike's approval because he not only held the keys to my future but also intentionally filled the gap in my life for a spiritual father. (Redman, 2024, at 14:21)

The Scolding Review added:

For many of those who have told their accounts to us, Mr Pilavachi's initial meeting with them was via the giving of so-called 'prophetic words' to them about their future or their lives, and so their encounters with Mr Pilavachi were imbued with and deeply entwined with their own faith and their views about Mr Pilavachi's ability to shape, influence or assist in the progression of that faith – which was also often intertwined with their employment and career paths. (Scolding and Fullbrook, 2024, p. 17)

Young men did their best to keep Pilavachi happy because they thought their careers depended on him. As these three examples demonstrate, the removal of agency through the control of career prospects is an all-too-common feature of spiritual abuse. This risk of loss of agency could be dealt with by much stronger channels of accountability. These would include education about appropriate behaviour, robust reporting of low-level concerns, complaints, whistleblowing policies and procedures, and oversight, including pastoral supervision. Of course, any of these measures could be gamed or ignored, but that is no reason not to implement them. It is notable that Scolding, Henderson and Fullbrook make similar points in relation to New Wine's responsibility to monitor Pilavachi's ongoing ministry (2025, p. 26).

Threatening a career is not the only form of fear-based control. Another aspect is bullying. The Fletcher Review found evidence of bullying in staff meetings. Similarly, a victim statement shown in the documentary *Let There Be Light* said:

> Over my years at Soul Survivor it was deeply painful and confusing to continually yo-yo from being in Mike's good books to being totally ousted. When you were being ignored and sidelined it was extremely painful and distressing. The impact of this wounded me deeply and caused considerable hurt and anguish that has lived with me for years. (Redman, 2024, at 1:43)

This type of unpredictable behaviour is one type of bullying that is often based on victim blaming, whereby the fear of ostracism enforces compliance. Living in highly unpredictable environments is disempowering, resulting in the loss of agency.

Michael Hall was also described as a bully:

> While Reverend Hall could be charming on occasion (the Diocese of Oxford received letters confirming this), he had mood swings and a temper. He was a physically imposing man who had boxed in his earlier life and his presence could be intimidating. There are several reports of Reverend Hall being physically aggressive towards others. He threw 'no parking' cones at a police officer, he punched a member of the congregation in the arm to prevent him from leaving a service, and there are reports of Reverend Hall hitting two people on separate occasions. (Hopkinson and Hopkinson, 2023, p. 7)

As well as these general observations, the Michael Hall case documents a specific form of bullying, namely threatening to take someone to court. In 1987, the patron of St Margaret's Church, Tylers Green, wanted to 'present' Hall to become the incumbent (vicar) for St Margaret's Church. However, having learned of Hall's bullying behaviour, the patron decided not to recommend him and, instead, sought his retirement on the grounds of ill health. Michael Hall refused to comply and commenced legal action.

> In March 1989 Reverend Hall's solicitors issued a writ against the patron for libel, slander and defamation. Shortly before the hearing that was due to be held in the High Court, at the suggestion of the patron, an out-of-court settlement was reached. (Hopkinson and Hopkinson, 2023, p. 13)

Hall's legal costs were paid by parishioners. It is unclear to me whether this was because they were afraid of him or because they genuinely thought he was hard done by. Although they must have been aware of the legal action, the senior staff of Oxford diocese did not raise any concerns. Does this indicate that even they were afraid of Hall? Bullying, or the threat of being bullied, is highly disempowering. Even those with theoretical power over the perpetrator can be bullied into complying.

It can be difficult to work out how to respond to bullying in the moment. The best strategies are formally documented ones. This requires having robust and rigorous processes that are implemented in an effective and timely fashion. The discussion of bystander programmes is relevant here. The Fletcher Review notes a culture of informality and disdain for processes. This created a culture in which bullying became an accepted norm and there were no objective means of challenging inappropriate behaviour (thirtyone:eight, 2021, p. 8).

Similarly, Pilavachi told the reviewers that the organizational structure of Soul Survivor was not fit for purpose:

> It was a 'bunch of friends' running a multi-million-pound organisation. Other trustees and those in positions of responsibility at various points from the early 1990s to the early 2020s did not disagree with that general view. The size, shape and scale of Soul Survivor required a more comprehensive framework of accountability, governance and oversight than was ever present. (Scolding and Fullbrook, 2024, p. 58)

This begs the question: if those with strategic and legal responsibility for Soul Survivor recognized these failures of governance, why did they do nothing to deal with the problem? (See also Scolding, Henderson and Fullbrook, 2025, pp. 25–37.)

Loss due to coercive control

The third aspect of loss of agency is coercive control, which is closely connected with bullying. As Hopkinson and Hopkinson explain:

> Reverend Hall's ministry has also been likened to a cult. Dissent was not allowed and those who were disloyal were targeted. Like a cult, it was hard to leave because Reverend Hall had made people dependent on him, and the penalties for getting out were potentially high. These included loss of friends and a sense of belonging, public denunciation, threat of litigation and (according to Reverend Hall) going to hell. Reverend Hall made people believe they could be 'struck down dead by God' at any given moment if they were 'not right with God', which parishioners understood to mean to be 'right' with Rev-

erend Hall. People were led to believe that the world would end during Reverend Hall's lifetime, which reinforced a cultist environment. (Hopkinson and Hopkinson, 2023, p. 16)

Coercive control is common in all the cases discussed in this chapter. Peter Ball controlled the young men who attended his quasi-monastic group, as well as those who lived with him while he was the Bishop of Lewes and subsequently the Bishop of Gloucester. Jonathan Fletcher had complete control over Emmanuel Church, Wimbledon. What he said was what happened (thirtyone:eight, 2021, pp. 7–9). The Makin Review documents similar deference to Smyth. Even when attempts were made to challenge or control Smyth's behaviour, he often had the last word. In 1982, a report known as the Ruston Report detailed the extent of Smyth's abusive behaviour. Those who read the report asked for Smyth's advice on how to respond, effectively leaving him in control of the situation (Makin, 2024, p. 233).

Similarly, Timothy Davis is described as a controlling and bullying individual who was not to be crossed. As the tribunal judgment notes, W2 found it difficult to challenge Davis because first, he was her boss; second, he backed up everything he said with Scripture; and third, Davis made it clear that God wanted his relationship with the family and the mentoring of W1 to continue (Church of England, 2017, p. 5).

The Home Office definition of coercive control states: 'Coercive behaviour is a continuing act or a pattern of acts of assault, threats, humiliation and intimidation or other abuse that is used to harm, punish, or frighten the victim' (Home Office, 2022a). This pattern is present in all the cases discussed here, although, apart from Smyth's horrific behaviour, incidents of physical assault are rare. Five of the perpetrators discussed appear to have relied more on manipulation, humiliation and intimidation.

Loss due to the perceived successful ministry of the perpetrator

The fourth aspect of loss of agency relates to the fact that these men were invariably regarded as 'successful' in their chosen branch of the Church. For example:

> JF was reported by some as an excellent teacher with a rare preaching gift. Under his leadership ECW was perceived by some as a very successful church, as the congregation grew significantly in number and profile. It was a place which became and remains a family to many. It also offered a home to those who wanted to explore Christianity intellectually. It undoubtedly provided solely positive experiences of church life for many who attended. (thirtyone:eight, 2021, p. 6)

Similarly, in the Pilavachi case – as Dr Amy Orr-Ewing argues in the documentary *Let There Be Light* – because Soul Survivor was perceived as so successful that there was 'a feeling of we wouldn't want to stop what the Lord [was] doing in some way, as if bringing challenge to terrible behaviour may in some way harm the kingdom'. This feeling led to a belief that, for the greater good, those who were abused 'need to get on with it [Christian ministry] and stop complaining or raising concerns' (Redman, 2024, at 16:01–16:25).

The review into this case suggests that success breeds blindness. The reviewers state:

> We have been given accounts by several people that, when they or others sought to bring difficulties and/or what they felt was unacceptable behaviour to the attention of people in positions of leadership, they were told that Mr Pilavachi's behaviour was to be excused because of the 'fruit of the ministry' that came from him or was not seen as 'that bad'. In other words, the unacceptable behaviours were a price to be paid for his gifts. (Scolding and Fullbrook, 2024, p. 50)

John Smyth had a reputation as a brilliant barrister and gifted preacher. His involvement with the Iwerne camps, which targeted boys at elite public schools, provided him with excellent cover for his abusive behaviour. As the Makin Review states, he was hidden in plain sight (Makin, 2024, pp. 235–7).

This fear of jeopardizing perceived success through the exposure of abuse deprives those who are abused of the ability to care for themselves, as their personal needs and well-being are ignored. Individuals are expected to submit to abuse for the sake of the perceived success of a ministry.

Success also comes by association:

> Peter Ball surrounded himself with powerful and influential friends. He had connections with members of parliament, headmasters of prominent public schools, Lord Lloyd of Berwick (who was a judge of the Court of Appeal at the time of Peter Ball's arrest and was subsequently a Law Lord) and [Charles] His Royal Highness the Prince of Wales. When Peter Ball was under police investigation, some of these persons of public prominence wrote in support of him. After he resigned, some of them encouraged his return to ministry and sought to assist him to do so. (IICSA, 2019, p. 111)

If the perpetrator is associated with powerful people, this robs victims of agency. It makes complaints and allegations appear unbelievable; it discourages people from raising concerns in the first place. While Smyth, Pilavachi, Fletcher and Ball were successful on the national stage, success at a local level can equally rob victims of agency. In the case of Timothy Davis, the reviewers comment on the difficulty of balancing the positive results of his long ministry at Christ Church, Abingdon, with the impact of his behaviour and actions on individuals (Lamb and Briden, 2020, p. 3). Similarly, Michael Hall enjoyed the support of the majority of his parochial church council (PCC), the governing body of the church (Hopkinson and Hopkinson, 2023, p. 37).

The risk of perceived success depriving people of agency is reduced primarily through thinking about what counts as success. The writers of the Fletcher Review said:

Question whether a church should continue to be defined as entirely successful given the information gathered around harmful behaviour experienced and the aspects of unhealthy culture that have been reported. (thirtyone:eight, 2021, p. 6)

In a Christian ministry context, a narrative of faithfulness and obedience can potentially help define success. But we must recognize that these concepts are equally open to misuse. The development of bystander programmes, and a healthy culture that recognizes 'it could happen here', would go some way towards reducing the risk of perceived success rendering people powerless to challenge inappropriate behaviour.

Loss due to the positive behaviours of the perpetrator

A fifth, related way in which individuals are deprived of agency concerns the perpetrator's positive behaviours. Thus, for example, Jonathan Fletcher was praised as a prolific letter writer, who regularly wrote to individuals to encourage them in their Christian life. This was one aspect of his 'personal work' of one-to-one support for young Christian men. He was also generous with financial gifts, providing lodging and accommodation for single men just starting out in ministry. Smyth established a similar persona. Peter Ball was praised as a talented preacher, with a gift for connecting with young people. Mike Pilavachi received similar praise for his generosity. In 2020, he was given the Alphege Award for Evangelism and Witness by the Archbishop of Canterbury. It was in recognition for his 'outstanding contribution to evangelism and discipleship amongst young people in the United Kingdom' (Church of England, 2020). The award has since been withdrawn.

The process of carefully and patiently establishing a trusted persona is a form of grooming. In these cases, it was not just the victim who was groomed into compliance, but the whole congregation, network or even the public. Parallels can be drawn with high-profile child sexual abuse cases, such as that of the UK television personality Jimmy Savile. Agency is not just lost by victims, but also by everyone who is touched by the abuse.

While discussing the Pilavachi case, Beth Redman said:

> You tried to stay because you were passionate about the people, and the mission and the ministry. And, you know, we loved Mike. We wanted to be in ministry with him. And what an amazing opportunity. And, so, you don't just walk away from those things easily. (Redman, 2024, at 13:24–13:42)

The ability of perpetrators to groom their victims to the point where the victim loves the perpetrator is an especially awful way of taking away agency. It can take decades to recover from and is difficult for outsiders to understand. Education on grooming is vital for restoring agency among all those impacted by abuse.

The reviewers of the Michael Hall case argue that his actions rendered both the Bishop of Buckingham and the Bishop of Oxford powerless; they also severely limited the power of the patron of St Margaret's. In the case of the patron, the reviewers are referring to the threats of legal action discussed on p. 81. Regarding the bishops, the Hall Review identifies four issues: the fear of Hall meant that those who were abused would not make their concerns public, which in turn meant that the bishops had no basis for action. Moreover, Hall's control of his congregation meant many, including most of the PCC, were loyal to him and distrustful of the diocese, thus further undermining any potential action by the bishops. Added to this was the threat of legal action and the lack of appropriate church legislation to deal with the issue (Hopkinson and Hopkinson, 2023, pp. 34–35).

Loss due to the assumption of a quasi-divine position

Finally, agency is lost when the perpetrator assumes a divine or quasi-divine position. As the reviewers note in the Hall case, Michael Hall

> would cite verses of the Bible to command obedience and suppress dissent. He expected the congregation to conform to his word, which he said was 'the word of God', and consequently to accept his spiritual leadership as absolute. (Hopkinson and Hopkinson, 2023, p. 7)

Smyth cited the Bible to justify his actions. Here are the words of one victim:

> I recall him talking to me in his study at Orchard House and he introduced the subject of a physical form of repentance by referring to scriptural verses from Hebrews and I believe from Samuel. He made specific references to marking your repentance by either shedding blood or I think there was a verse that talks about stripes on your body. John Smyth used these verses to suggest to us that the time had come in our spiritual growth to begin to show proper repentance for the sins that we were committing. (Makin, 2024, p. 45)

Arguably, Peter Ball also assumed a quasi-divine position. For example:

> When he was 16 years old, AN-A102 sought pastoral guidance from Peter Ball. Peter Ball asked him to remove his clothing and stand naked in front of the vestry mirror which, he said, was a metaphor for the eyes of God. Peter Ball claimed this would help him to find humility. (IICSA, 2019, p. 117)

Scolding and Fullbrook note that many considered Pilavachi to have a special relationship with God that must not be interfered with in any way (Scolding and Fullbrook, 2024, pp. 49–50). Referring to the reluctance of victims to disclose abuse, Dr Diane Langberg explained that

> they would be going against everyone to speak the truth and leave and so they doubt themselves. The other piece is that there is a dynamic with an abuser and a victim and there are ways in which the victim feels special, important, part of a big work. 'And yes, I get that [that you're experiencing abuse] but you wouldn't want to destroy God's work, would you? You're a part of God's work' ... It's not that they're going to deal with somebody who's abusive. They're going to bring down God's work and they can't do that. (Redman, 2024, at 11:31–12:14)

This claiming divine status is especially damaging, as it goes to the core of personal identity. The perpetrator assumes a status 'as God' to the victim and, as such, the victim becomes unable to resist, for to resist would be to destroy their faith.

In this section, I have discussed six interrelated aspects of how spiritual abuse deprives the abused of agency. While the focus was mainly on those who are directly abused, it should be noted that they are not the only people who are deprived of agency. Their family, friends and bystanders are also affected. Steps must be taken to enable a greater development of agency at least partly through education, a topic to which I now turn.

Education

This section will examine five aspects of education concerning spiritual abuse. First, the use of reviews for learning. Second, the need for, but lack of, basic education around safeguarding. Third, the need for appropriate terminology. Fourth, the need for education as to what constitutes spiritual abuse. Fifth, education includes the need for policies, procedures and space for protection.

The first point to note is that reading and engaging with reviews of spiritual abuse is an education in and of itself. If you read the reviews and take the lessons on board, you are less likely to abuse others and are better equipped to identify and respond to abuse if you encounter it. The use of the Peter Ball case within Anglican safeguarding training is a relevant example. Arguably, all religious leaders should be expected to engage with lessons-learned reviews as part of their ongoing safeguarding training and professional development.

Second, there is a need for basic education in relation to safeguarding and to develop an understanding and a culture that recognizes 'it could happen here'. While discussing the Hall case, the reviewers comment:

Today, churchwardens and the PCC would be expected to recognise the warning signs of abuse and to make sure it is reported to the diocese. During Reverend Hall's time at St Margaret's Church this does not appear to have been the case. (Hopkinson and Hopkinson, 2023, p. 22)

While this is the reviewers' expectation, it is not necessarily true. In her account of abuse by Pilavachi, Beth Redman details her ignorance about the existence of the Church of England National Safeguarding Team (Redman, 2024, at 22:43). Scolding and Fullbrook document the lack of understanding of safeguarding at Soul Survivor, as well as the fact that Pilavachi did not receive proper training before or after he was ordained (Scolding and Fullbrook, 2024, pp. 40–5, 74–5). Timothy Davis received no safeguarding training in more than two decades at Christ Church, Abingdon (Lamb and Briden, 2020, 12). Similarly, the Fletcher Review notes that

> the safeguarding audit and interviews demonstrated a lack of policy, process and procedure in place within ECW during JF's period as Vicar. In addition, a celebration of informality, a lack of recording or confidentiality and the lack of value placed on safeguarding undermined confidence in being able to disclose or raise concerns. (thirtyone:eight, 2021, p. 8)

A lack of education about safeguarding results in a culture that is dismissive of concerns and has no conception that 'it could happen here'. Beth Redman describes meeting with 'a senior church leader in London' and disclosing that Pilavachi was massaging interns dressed only in their underwear. The response 'not dismissively or unkindly, just matter of fact, was "That's just Mike. Nothing will be done"' (Redman, 2024, at 18:04–18:47). The same sort of reaction, that it was 'just Fletch' or 'just Fletcher', is highlighted by the reviewers (thirtyone:eight, 2021, pp. 38 and 53). While this exact phrase is not used by the IICSA investigation, reference is made to the fact that Peter Ball had been told 'no more boys', which indicates a similar attitude (IICSA, 2019, p. 122). Similarly, John Smyth was allowed to move to Africa even though his abusive practices were known. In all these cases, the existence of a culture that recognized that spiritual abuse occurs, and that any concerns should be investigated thoroughly, would have gone a long way towards reducing the risk of abuse.

The third point the reviews make in relation to education is the importance of correct terminology and, by extension, of developing a clearer understanding of who might be affected by spiritual abuse. Two reviews raised concern over the use of the term 'vulnerable'. Hopkinson and Hopkinson, while recognizing that 'vulnerable' is used in some legislation, stated:

> There is a risk that would-be complainants or whistle-blowers may not understand what a vulnerable adult is or recognise themselves to be one. To encourage people to come forward about abuse, it might be more inclusive to replace references to 'vulnerable adults' with 'adults experiencing or at risk of abuse', except where appropriate in relation to the barred lists. (Hopkinson and Hopkinson, 2023, pp. 31–2)

The Fletcher Review argues for greater thought about what constitutes vulnerability. The writers explained that the review

> demonstrates that current understandings of safeguarding primarily are seen to relate to children, young people and adults 'at risk of harm' (often still referred to in faith contexts as vulnerable). Where adults do not meet the criteria for being at risk of harm, they can experience damaging behaviours that do not cross into a statutory category of harm and in this context can render them vulnerable. There is a need for this current void to be addressed. There has rightly been recognition that in cases of domestic violence, experiences of coercive control are categorised as abusive and constitute a legal offence. However, this does not currently apply outside of the intimate partner or family context.
>
> We also consider that the issue of consent requires further legislative scrutiny in contexts where there is a significant imbalance of power and/or status and/or age including in a religious context. (thirtyone:eight, 2021, p. 100)

This recommendation is a challenging one. The debate as to when and how people become 'vulnerable' or 'at risk' is complex. When considering the cases discussed, the evidence suggests Neil Todd was vulnerable and at risk of harm by Peter Ball; similarly with W1 in relation to Timothy Davis. But were all Pilavachi's interns at risk, or those who worked at Emmanuel Church, Wimbledon? I am not able to comment on these specifics; but I wonder whether it is appropriate to assume that because someone experienced abuse, they must have been at risk or vulnerable. This returns us to the question of subjectivity. Who defines what constitutes abuse? The Fletcher case is especially relevant, given some experienced his behaviours but did not regard them as abusive (thirtyone:eight, 2021, p. 5).

I do not have the expertise to comment on what a potential legal definition might be. But I note IICSA recommendation 3:

> The government should amend Section 21 of the Sexual Offences Act 2003 so as to include clergy within the definition of a position of trust. This would criminalise under s16–s20 sexual activity between clergy and a person aged 16–18, over whom they exercise pastoral authority, involving the abuse of a position of trust.

This seems relevant to the point made in the Fletcher Review: namely, that we should broaden the scope of who is considered to be at risk of being harmed by spiritual abuse. I should, however, point out that the IICSA recommendation is specifically in reference to sexual activity, which is not present in all the cases discussed here. Legally defining spiritual abuse remains a complex task.

Fourth, the review of the Michael Hall case argues for education as to what constitutes spiritual abuse. The reviewers note that, during Hall's ministry, terminology concerning spiritual abuse was not in common use. It was therefore difficult for those who were abused by Hall to develop an appropriate language for and response to their experiences (Hopkinson and Hopkinson, 2023, p. 16). Moreover, as the reviewers explain, one of the challenges inherent in identifying spiritual abuse is that it can be misinterpreted as passionately held, compassionate beliefs. This can lead to a lack of inquisitiveness and an overly optimistic hope that problems will resolve themselves since such convictions may not necessarily be considered harmful. They may in fact be mistaken for strong and firm faith. Consequently, as the Church of England Safeguarding e-manual makes clear, attention should be given to the impact of beliefs, convictions and ministry and how they are being, or might be, used to psychologically, financially, sexually or physically harm others. (Hopkinson and Hopkinson, 2023, p. 34)

We must plan carefully to help people to learn about spiritual abuse. A good place to start is with the Hall Review's recommendations regarding briefing sessions, the production of posters and the use of Safeguarding Sunday as an annual reminder of the risks of spiritual abuse (Hopkinson and Hopkinson, 2023, p. 37).

But posters and an annual sermon will not change organizational culture by themselves: that requires deeper, sustained effort. Among other points, Scolding and Fullbrook suggested that those in leadership at Soul Survivor develop a more open, less defensive leadership culture, and that more robust procedures for handling complaints are put in place and communicated clearly (Scolding and Fullbrook, 2024, p. 89).

The Fletcher Review makes numerous recommendations in this regard, including for the development of an action plan for Emmanuel Church, Wimbledon. Such a plan will

> ensure there is teaching developing a healthy culture and the hallmarks of this and to include material on bullying, manipulation, coercive control and spiritual abuse as part of this to raise awareness of these behaviours and their impact and to explore best practice for response in order to create a healthy culture in which these behaviours are more likely to be recognised and responded to effectively in the future. (thirtyone:eight, 2021, p. 92)

This will also require reflection on what it means to lead in a church context, including a review of leadership structures, thinking about leadership styles and individual behaviour, and receiving 'healthy leadership training delivered by organizations beyond the current constituency'. In addition, the reviewers recommend the following:

- a review of the process for appointing elders
- regular meetings between churchwardens and the vicar to provide appropriate support and challenge
- a communication strategy for engaging with the wider congregation
- the development and dissemination of a low-level concerns policy
- strengthening relationships with the diocese
- staff commitment to the appraisal process
- the possible establishment of an external body to handle complaints
- work to ensure any mission agencies the church engages with have appropriate safeguarding policies and procedures. (thirtyone:eight, 2021, pp. 93–94)

This is a long list of changes to be implemented. It will require significant investment of time and resources. It will be successful only if those concerned buy into it; and commitment will come only if people understand why these things are necessary. Education about the risks and realities of spiritual abuse is therefore the foundation upon which the development of a healthy culture can be built.

It is never too early to begin education about spiritual abuse. The Fletcher Review makes this recommendation:

> Those organisations that provide ministry training should consider developing reflective practice in ministry around power, positioning and influence in their local context and across contexts in which they minister and allow external scrutiny of leadership. (thirtyone:eight, 2021, p. 97)

The continuum developed by Professor Oakley (see pp. 17–18) is a useful tool for reflection – both for individuals and in a group-supervision context. Similarly, education about pastoral supervision, including on how to be supervised, would reduce the risk of inadvertent harm.

Finally, education must include the raising of awareness as to how to report concerns or make a formal complaint. The Hall Review recognizes it is difficult for victims to come forward; it therefore recommends that responsible bodies 'ensure that guidance on how to complain is clear, understandable, and unambiguous, and that there are no inadvertent barriers that may deter a victim from seeking help'. This includes ensuring the national guidance on the CDM process is as accessible as possible (Hopkinson and Hopkinson 2023, p. 32). The CDM has been replaced by the Clergy Conduct Measure (CCM), but the same point applies. After all, it is only if appropriate pathways are available that people can find the support they need if they have experienced spiritual abuse.

Connections with my conversations

This section discusses the connections between my analysis of the Church of England accounts of spiritual abuse and the conversations I had with Christians, Hindus, Jews, Muslims and Sikhs. As noted in the ethical discussion above, references to participants are vague to preserve their anonymity.

Agency

First, no interviewee made a direct comment on the process-driven loss of agency. However, many of them did raise concerns about the impact of the police or social services investigating spiritual abuse. I take this to be an indirect indication of the fear that, were such bodies to be involved in investigating spiritual abuse, it is highly possible, if not probable, that victims would experience a process-driven loss of agency. As noted on p. 30, a participant asked, 'How do you bring in a statutory agency that's dealing with, actually, people's deep, deep rooted, well, beliefs and spirituality?' Another participant suggested that the authorities might take things out of context or misunderstand; they said, 'Sometimes, when something's handed over to the law, an issue that could have quite easily been resolved becomes fixed, and then it becomes, you know, irreconcilable.' These are but two examples of how participants hinted at their fear of a process-driven loss of agency.

Second, reference was made to a fear-based loss of agency. A Sikh participant discussed their fear of actions that might be taken by a guru and his followers.

> People [could use] the religion or belief to coerce or push or bully other people. And that's simply about [saying], 'I'm now taking upon myself the responsibility of being, you know, judge, jury, executioner, or the enforcer of what the faith teaches, and what I'm saying, what I believe is precisely what everyone else must believe.'

Similarly, a Hindu participant talked about their fear of the mandir (temple) committee stifling criticism and challenge.

Third, a Jewish participant discussed religiously based coercive control; they made a specific reference to a husband preventing his wife from fulfilling religious obligations, such as making challah for the Shabbat evening meal. Other examples included restrictions as to what clothing is worn, as well as what education is received. It was noted that significant portions of Jewish faith and practice are based at home, which creates a potential environment for domestic abuse, with an element of spiritual abuse.

Fourth, the notion of perceived success preventing a perpetrator from being challenged was not directly referenced. However, there was discussion of 'clericalism', including the Anglo-Catholic attitude of 'Father knows best'. A similar point was made by a Hindu participant. This is likely to manifest in unhealthy or perhaps merely unhelpful behaviours rather than abuse. But excessive deference does potentially establish foundations upon which abuse can be built.

A participant discussed the way in which people wittingly or unwittingly engage with people offering faith healing, or who offer to solve marriage or financial problems. The perception that these people are successful in providing what they offer leads vulnerable and naive individuals to engage in risky behaviour and to accept abusive practices.

Fifth, at least one participant referred to an individual's positive behaviour resulting in loss of agency. The context was of recognizing that a spiritual leader was behaving inappropriately towards young female devotees. Most followers held their leader in such high regard that they could not conceive of his doing anything wrong. The focus groups discussed the cost of speaking out. In a tightly knit religious community or faith-based organization, however much anonymity is promised, the reality is that whistleblowers are likely to be identified and experience pushback, challenge or even threats to their lives.

Sixth, the idea of someone assuming a divine position did occur. A participant stated that people 'may incrementally recognize, over time, that they have influence and, over time, maybe lose sight of that which the faith teaches, and they become enamoured in their own power, and almost become God-like themselves'. This concept was discussed in the focus groups under the theme of 'divinified control' and the idea of 'false saints' or 'false gurus'. While most participants in the follow-up discussions did not find this language helpful, some did. Moreover, it does resonate with my analysis of the Church of England cases.

Education

Turning to the discussion of education, it is difficult to identify precisely the five themes in the conversations (see p. 89), but there are many points of connection. First, the reviews are useful for learning. As the learning from a Methodist Past Cases Review found, there is plenty that can be learned from the mistakes of the past (Methodist Church, 2016). But sadly, these lessons do not necessarily have an impact on practice because the connection with current actions is not necessarily made.

Second, 13 of the 15 participants in the first phase of my research talked about the importance of training and education. Three referred to policies and procedures, confirming the need to establish appropriate systems. There was debate as to the balance of internal and external input, but the fundamental issue was the need for people to become more alert to the possibility of spiritual abuse.

Third, there is a need for appropriate terminology. A participant made an observation that is relevant to the debate about vulnerability and being 'at risk': namely, that people can have radically different understandings and reflections on the same experiences. While one individual may categorically state that they were vulnerable and abused, someone else might describe the same actions of the same leader as profoundly helpful for their own spiritual development.

Fourth, education as to what constitutes spiritual abuse. The follow-up interviews focused on the importance of survivor testimonies, used carefully, together with an open, non-confrontational style of delivery. I have adopted the approach to training that 'the journey is the destination' in this regard. I offer workshop participants a range of definitions and scenarios to discuss that allow them to develop their own understandings. There are, of course, limits. Some behaviour is unacceptable. But as one Hindu participant noted, consulting with one's guru about a minor decision might be a healthy spiritual practice for some but, for others, would be an unhelpful indication of unnecessary accountability. Not all cases are clear cut.

Fifth, education includes the need for policies, procedures and space for reflection. The idea of pastoral supervision received qualified support from the participants; it can help, provided it is balanced with appropriate accountability. The references to peer mentoring, closed social media groups and the development of self-reflection are all important.

So what?

The six documented cases have been examined in detail by experts, while, in the main, my interviewees did not classify themselves as people who had experienced spiritual abuse; nor were they experts in responding to it. This is an important finding in and of itself, demonstrating that while most people of faith may not have personal encounters with spiritual abuse, they nevertheless have an instinctive understanding of what abusive behaviour looks like.

There are also clear connections between the reviews and the theory of agency and education developed from the conversations and focus groups. Reflection on the six cases led to my developing a six-strand theory of loss of agency, which also connected with the conversations. Similarly, the five aspects of education, discussed on pages 89–93, also connected with my research, but in a less precise manner. Hopefully, my detailed discussion of the reviews has shed further light on the theory of agency and education.

Finally, there is the question of institutional inertia, cover-up and unwillingness to take issues of spiritual abuse seriously. I have not discussed this because of my decision to focus primarily on individual experiences. It does leave a significant gap in my argument. While I recognize that changing the culture of religious institutions is important, I think the best way to do so is to empower and educate individuals.

6

Faith, Power and Abuse: A Christian Reflection

[Timothy Davis] under the guise of his authority sought to control by the use of admonition, Scripture, prayer and revealed prophecy the life of W1 and/or his relationship with his girlfriend. (Church of England, 2017, p. 2)

In this chapter, I reflect theologically, from an Anglican Christian perspective, on the causes and consequences of spiritual abuse. While much of this book contains interreligious perspectives on spiritual abuse, I am a Christian and believe it is appropriate to reflect as a Christian on the issues. As with Chapter 5, this one will be of most benefit to Anglican Christians. But I hope there is food for thought for those of other religions and no religion who have an interest in safeguarding and preventing abuse.

This chapter is divided into six parts: first, two words of caution; second, a reflection on the theory of agency and education; third, a discussion of texts in the Hebrew Scriptures; fourth, Jesus' rebuke of religious leaders; fifth, Paul's concerns about the believers in Galatia; and sixth, reflections on how we should lead.

Two words of caution

When we read and discuss the Bible, it is easy to spot only the bits with which we agree and to avoid inconvenient truths. What about the passages that we find difficult? One participant referenced the use of Malachi 3.8–12 in the context of encouraging financial giving. The text reads:

FAITH, POWER AND ABUSE: A CHRISTIAN REFLECTION

Will anyone rob God? Yet you are robbing me! But you say, 'How are we robbing you?' In your tithes and offerings! You are cursed with a curse, for you are robbing me – the whole nation of you! Bring the full tithe into the storehouse, so that there may be food in my house, and thus put me to the test, says the Lord of hosts; see if I will not open the windows of heaven for you and pour down for you an overflowing blessing. I will rebuke the locust for you, so that it will not destroy the produce of your soil; and your vine in the field shall not be barren, says the Lord of hosts. Then all nations will count you happy, for you will be a land of delight, says the Lord of hosts.

Is it spiritual abuse if a preacher quotes this text and teaches that we are irrevocably cursed if we do not tithe or that we will receive abundant blessing if we give sacrificially? Teaching on this text may be unhelpful, or even healthy, depending on how the topic is discussed and the level of pressure that is put upon the congregation. It might be used to enforce tithing or as part of an open invitation to reflect on personal generosity.

Similarly, the command that wives submit to their husbands in Ephesians 5.22, if taken out of context, can be used to justify abusive behaviours. Similar arguments could be made about other texts, but the point is clear. We must take care when reading and teaching Scripture.

We should also avoid antisemitism. It would be easy, but wrong, to read some passages of the Hebrew Scriptures and the New Testament as saying that 'the Jews' engaged in abusive practices and Christians did not. This is, of course, a wholly inadequate and inaccurate way of reading the texts. I have written at length elsewhere about this issue, specifically in reference to Matthew's and John's Gospels (Wilson, 2020; Wilson, 2022), so I will not repeat myself here. It is worth flagging the risk and suggesting some useful books for those who want to read more about Christian antisemitism (Bayfield, 2017; Le Donne and Behrendt, 2017; Levine, 2006; Levine and Brettler, 2020).

Agency and education

The Bible has much to say about both agency and education. Considering education, Christians are disciples of Jesus Christ. Other words for 'disciple' are 'student' and 'learner'. To be a Christian is to commit to learning about how to live life in all its fullness, modelling your life on the thoughts and actions of Jesus Christ. All Christians are therefore committed to learning, and this includes understanding how Christianity can be abused to harm other people.

The Book of Proverbs includes many references to education, mainly in a home context; it urges parents to bring up their children to be faith filled and faith directed, and to develop their lives on the wisdom of the Hebrew Scriptures. Jesus taught through parables and stories, as well as through dialogue and questions. Sometimes Jesus gives very blunt and direct answers to specific questions, but often he responds to a question with a question or with a story that is open to interpretation and discussion. An open-ended style of education and use of creative methods fits with the approach taken by Jesus.

But what about those who want to be teachers? Acts 13.1 mentions teachers and prophets in the early Christian community at Antioch; they are included in the order 'first apostles, second prophets, third teachers' (1 Cor. 12.28), as well as in other lists (Eph. 4.11; 1 Tim. 2.7; 2 Tim. 1.11). These texts all indicate that the teacher is under special authority from God, but there is no exact definition of the role or responsibility. In James 3.1, those who teach are warned that they will be judged more strictly because of their greater responsibility. Teachers have a specific, God-given task of instruction, so others ought to listen to them. For example, the 108 verses of James contain 54 commands (Baker, 1995, p. 6). James does not urge or persuade; he instructs his readers in the correct course of action to follow. James assumes an authority that is not open to question; he expects his audience to recognize and acknowledge his position and so obey his teaching.

FAITH, POWER AND ABUSE: A CHRISTIAN REFLECTION

Turning to agency, both the Hebrew Scriptures and the New Testament teach individual accountability and responsibility for action. A clear example is found in Ezekiel 18:

> The word of the Lord came to me: What do you mean by repeating this proverb concerning the land of Israel, 'The parents have eaten sour grapes, and the children's teeth are set on edge'? As I live, says the Lord God, this proverb shall no more be used by you in Israel. Know that all lives are mine; the life of the parent as well as the life of the child is mine: it is only the person who sins that shall die. (vv. 1–4)

This is not the first time in the Hebrew Scriptures that individual responsibility is discussed. Both passages containing the Ten Commandments warn of punishment for iniquity to the third or fourth generation (Ex. 20.4–5; Deut. 5.9–10). The Lord makes the same point when he passes before Moses (Ex. 34.6–7). The history books also teach that the generations they record were being punished for the actions of their ancestors (2 Kings 22.13; 23.26; 24.3–4). Unfaithfulness develops over generations, resulting in unavoidable punishment (Lee, 2021, pp. 44–6).

The 'sour grapes' proverb is also found in Jeremiah 31.29; scholars debate the connection between the two. Both prophets have the same aim in mind: 'To give their audiences the means to survive their present circumstances' (Lee, 2021, p. 44). Those to whom Ezekiel is speaking are fatalistic. They think that it is because of their ancestors' sins that they are being punished with exile; they believe that there is nothing they themselves can do about it. This is not the case. The crucial statement is in Ezekiel 18.19: a negative question that argues the son should not suffer for the iniquity of the father. Ezekiel's audience believe that they, the sons, are suffering because of the fathers' actions. Ezekiel argues against this. The past does not determine the evaluation of those in the present. If they choose to do what is right, then they will live; but if they remain in sin and rebellion, they will die (Lee, 2021, pp. 46–8).

In Jeremiah, the focus is on God's promise to transform Israel's hearts, overturning the inevitability of sinfulness and bringing about a better future (Jeremiah 31.27–40). Jeremiah's use of the sour grapes proverb is as reassurance that the day is coming when the current generation will not suffer the consequences of their ancestors' sin. Jeremiah agrees with his audience that transgenerational retribution is currently in operation. But he disagrees with their belief that this is an everlasting situation. God will bring in a day when transgenerational retribution no longer occurs (Lee, 2021, pp. 48–50).

While Ezekiel and Jeremiah disagree as to whether the sour grapes proverb accurately describes their audiences' situation, they agree that the proverb does not provide a helpful pathway to survival (Lee, 2021, p. 52). God provides a way forward for his people, who must listen to his voice and follow where he leads them.

> The exiles are in a transitory period between life and death and must choose the generation with which they will identify. (Strine, 2012, p. 478)

The decision is for individuals and for the whole nation. There is scope therefore for individual agency even within group responsibility. The sinful generation were punished with exile. The current generation, their children, must choose whether to associate themselves with their ancestors' sin or with the new future that God has promised. Perhaps the true parable would be, 'Your teeth will stop being set on edge when you stop eating sour grapes' (Mitchell, 2017, p. 86).

In other words, our actions have consequences; but God also acts, and we should join with him. The Apostle Paul makes a similar point when he urges the believers in Philippi to 'work out your own salvation with fear and trembling; for it is God who is at work in you, enabling you both to will and to work for his good pleasure' (Phil. 2.12–13). People have individual responsibility and agency, but God is also at work within them. And as with the Ezekiel passage, there is both an individual and a group aspect: 'the community helping one another to work out their personal salvation' (Witherington, 2011, p. 159).

FAITH, POWER AND ABUSE: A CHRISTIAN REFLECTION

People have agency, but that does not make them personally responsible for everything that happens to them, which John 9 highlights:

> As he [Jesus] walked along, he saw a man blind from birth. His disciples asked him, 'Rabbi, who sinned, this man or his parents, that he was born blind?' Jesus answered, 'Neither this man nor his parents sinned; he was born blind so that God's works might be revealed in him. We must work the works of him who sent me while it is day; night is coming when no one can work'. (vv. 1–4)

The Disciples seem to suggest the sinfulness of the man's parents was the cause of his blindness (Thomaskutty, 2022, p. 2). But Jesus is clear that 'sin is not the reason for the man's predicament' (Michaels, 2010, p. 541).

What does this passage teach us about the nature of God? If the traditional punctuation is followed, it implies that God is cruel, causing the man to suffer for his whole life as a blind person solely for this one moment when Jesus heals him. Perhaps we need different punctuation? John Poirier suggests we put the full stop much earlier in verse 3. If so, the passage would read:

> Jesus answered, 'Neither this man nor his parents sinned so that he was born blind. But in order that God's works might be revealed in him, we must work the works of him who sent me while it is day; night is coming when no one can work'. (Poirier, 2010, p. 61)

If we follow this suggestion, Jesus denies the claim that human sinfulness causes blindness; he does not link the man's blindness to direct divine intervention. Then Jesus begins a new sentence, about the urgency of the healing. It must be carried out *now*, so the people can see it taking place. There may also be a hint that the healing should be completed *today*, while it is still the Sabbath, before night comes and a new day begins (Poirier, 2010, p. 62). John Poirier's point that God is not cruel or vindictive is important for how we understand agency. It is not that we have no agency. Fatalism – the belief we have no control over our lives and deserve bad things – has no place in Christianity. But the same is true of the belief that we are free agents who control everything. We are accountable for our actions, but not everything that happens to us is our personal responsibility.

We need to strike a balance between personal agency and divine sovereignty. The concept of personal accountability and judgement by God is clear within the New Testament. In 2 Corinthians 5.10, Paul writes, 'For all of us must appear before the judgement seat of Christ, so that each may receive recompense for what has been done in the body, whether good or evil.' Paul 'reminds us that we have been saved, not for a life of aimlessness or indifference, but to live as to the Lord' (Barnett, 1997, p. 277).

This notion of personal accountability is perhaps nowhere clearer than in the parables and warnings of Matthew 25. The chapter is divided into three parts. First, the parable of the wise and foolish virgins reminds the audience that the timing of Christ's return is unknown, but believers should nevertheless get ready. No explanation is given as to why the bridegroom is delayed. All we know is that he is and that all ten young women fall asleep. When the bridegroom eventually turns up, only five have made adequate preparations and can join in with the procession and the wedding feast, the highlight of the celebration.

> The point is simply that readiness, whatever form it takes, is not something that can be achieved by a last-minute adjustment. It depends on long-term provision, and if that has been made, the wise disciple can sleep secure in the knowledge that everything is ready. (France, 2007, p. 947)

The fact is that individual choice determines how people respond to God's kingdom. To fail to be adequately prepared is an insult to the bride and groom, which is why the unprepared are rejected and excluded (Keener, 1999, pp. 597–9).

Second, the idea behind the parable of the slaves entrusted with money (Matt. 25.14–30) is the necessity of maximizing opportunities, being focused and working, and not worrying about the timing of the Lord's return. The parable is not about individual ability, but 'the specific privileges and opportunities of the kingdom of heaven and the responsibilities they entail' (France, 2007, p. 951). This means that the exclusion of the third servant is 'the punishment for a professed disciple who failed to invest all his or her resources in the work of the kingdom' (Keener, 1999, p. 602).

Third, Matthew 25.31–46, the passage that foretells Christ's return and judgement of all people, explains that those who have lived according to the will of God will be rewarded, while those who have not will be punished. But the main point is the sovereignty of God (France, 2007, p. 959).

All three sections of Matthew 25 reinforce the idea about agency and accountability discussed above. To live as a Christian is to make choices not simply for one's own good, but for the good of all. Jesus 'called the crowd with his disciples, and said to them, "If any want to become my followers, let them deny themselves and take up their cross and follow me"' (Mark 8.34; see also Matthew 16.24 and Luke 9.23). True agency for the Christian is therefore rooted in denial of self in the cause of obedience to Christ and service of others.

Warnings from the Hebrew Scriptures

This section discusses four passages: Leviticus 10, Jeremiah 36, Ezekiel 34 and Amos 5. Leviticus 10 recounts how

> Aaron's sons, Nadab and Abihu, each took his censer, put fire in it, and laid incense on it; and they offered unholy fire before the Lord, such as he had not commanded them. And fire came out from the presence of the Lord and consumed them, and they died before the Lord. (vv. 1–2)

Scholars debate the nature of the 'unholy fire'. One scholar refers to it as 'strange fire', fire from an improper source (Houston, 2000, p. 33). There are many possible interpretations of what the problem was, including improper timing, inappropriate zeal or lack of ritual purity; or that Nadab and Abihu were not ordained priests or that they offered private incense (Bibb, 2001, pp. 85–6). It is difficult to decide which is correct, for 'the text resists attempts to determine what Nadab and Abihu did wrong' (Heyd, 2022, p. 552). Is the focus of the narrative on Aaron's obedience and not on his sons? Aaron does not mourn, and remains ritually pure, thereby ensuring the Lord's honour is secure.

Perhaps the point is that Nadab and Abihu were given no instruction by God. Does 'such as he had not commanded them' indicate an absence of the Lord's command, not a prohibition? Is the point not that they broke a rule, but that they acted without clear instructions? 'They are living within the gap, searching for the presence of Yahweh, stumbling blindly in the dark' (Bibb, 2001, p. 89). In this reading, Nadab and Abihu attempt to stand before a holy God based on their own instincts but fail and are punished. The rest of Leviticus shows Moses learning how to stand before God without experiencing punishment. 'The story does not just *have* gaps. It is *about* gaps and how we deal with them' (Bibb, 2001, p. 98). It warns us of the risks and realities of operating in the dark.

Nadab and Abihu receive no direct command from God, and act without clear knowledge of what the correct course of action is. This idea of operating in the gaps, with no certainty that what one is doing is right, helps us to think about the reality of spiritual abuse. As noted above, while some set out to manipulate and harm, others accidently abuse or act unhealthily. Whether the abuse is intentional or inadvertent, Leviticus 10 reminds us of the holiness of God and the standards of behaviour required, even if the detail is not always clear.

Jeremiah 36 also features fire, although in this case it is a brazier. The prophet is commanded by God to write the prophecies he has received about the fate of Judah, Israel and the nations on a scroll. Baruch records all that Jeremiah dictates, then takes the scroll to the temple, where a fast is declared and the people listen to Baruch reading out the scroll. Baruch is then asked to read the scroll to the king's officials. They report to Jehoakim, the king.

> Then the king sent Jehudi to get the scroll, and he took it from the chamber of Elishama the secretary; and Jehudi read it to the king and all the officials who stood beside the king. Now the king was sitting in his winter apartment (it was the ninth month), and there was a fire burning in the brazier before him. As Jehudi read three or four columns, the king would cut them off with a penknife and throw them into the fire in the brazier, until the entire scroll was consumed in the fire that was in the brazier. Yet neither the king, nor any of his servants who heard all these words, was alarmed, nor did they tear their garments. (Jer. 36.21–4)

When he burns the scroll, Jehoakim both symbolizes the destruction of Judah and brings it about through his actions. He rejects the prophecy signified by the scroll, and so rejects God, which in turn makes punishment inevitable (Deken, 2017, p. 631). The specific act of rejecting the scroll and burning it is a metaphor for the breakdown of the relationship between Judah and the Lord. The whole of Jeremiah (and indeed many of the other prophets) gives further evidence of the breakdown in the relationship between God and his people. Jeremiah 36 reminds us that actions have consequences, both for individuals and for society. Spiritual abuse never impacts just one or two individuals. As the Church of England case studies demonstrated, whole congregations were negatively affected because of the inappropriate actions of a single leader. Although we cannot argue from Jeremiah 36 for the destruction of a nation because of sinful disobedience, we can sound a clear warning that individual actions ripple out and potentially hurt many.

Amos 5 is another oracle of judgement. Amos speaks here of Israel's relationship with God, centred on the themes of death and life, and worship and justice (Jeremias, 1998, pp. 83–4). Amos challenges hypocritical, self-centred religion, which is full of meaningless ritual and lacks authenticity, as society is blighted by social injustice (Groenewald, 2019, p. 6). Amos 5.18–27 speaks of divine disgust and anger towards Israelite behaviour (Jeremias, 1998, p. 98). Empty worship is rejected as meaningless. The justice and righteousness the Lord expects should be natural for the people of God. Righteousness is primarily relational, acting for the good of a community, flowing from a right relationship with the Lord (Jeremias, 1998, pp. 103–4).

Amos criticizes outward religiosity that lacks substance, and hypocritical religious action that masks exploitation and greed. These also feature in the Church of England case studies discussed in Chapter 5. Peter Ball, for example, was considered a pious and holy man, yet he used this image as a front to enable him to sexually abuse vulnerable young men and boys. Similar points could be made about the other case studies, but it is unnecessary to repeat the detail here.

Ezekiel 34 contrasts good and bad shepherds as a metaphor for the leadership of the people of God. The idea of leader as shepherd is a common one in the Hebrew Bible and is found in Psalm 23, 2 Samuel 5.2, Isaiah 40.11 and Jeremiah 23.1–4, as well as Ezekiel 34 (Resane, 2014, p. 1). Moses (Isa. 63.11) and David (Ps. 78.70–1) are referred to as shepherd leaders. In Zechariah 10–11, the Lord explains why his anger is 'hot against the shepherds' (White, 2021, p. 5). Thomas Resane suggests that there are three main functions of a shepherd. First, caring, which includes restoration, feeding, watering, grooming, shearing, delivering lambs, leading and protecting. The second requirement is for courage: assuming responsibility for the sheep, both serving and challenging as necessary. Third, guidance: keeping them safe and directing them to an appropriate destination. The bad shepherds of Ezekiel 34 have completely failed to fulfil these functions (Resane, 2014, pp. 2–6).

Amy White reflects on Ezekiel 34 as she develops a theological definition of spiritual abuse. The Hebrew Scriptures characterize God as the true shepherd of his people. White argues that when leaders are described as shepherds 'they in some way point to God in their shepherding, whether positively or negatively' (White, 2021, p. 5). This means that bad shepherds do not merely have an impact on the health of the sheep. They also damage the understanding of God as divine Shepherd.

Who are the bad shepherds? Based on her reading of Ezekiel, White proposes both religious and civic leaders are included. The bad shepherds are kings, princes, officials, prophets, priests and elders. The society addressed by Ezekiel is completely rotten:

> Wherever a power imbalance was in operation there was opportunity for abuse, and in a society where all strata of leadership had abandoned the ways of the Lord for their own gain, those opportunities were very often seized. (White, 2021, p. 6)

Spiritual abuse is like yeast: 'A little of which affects the whole lump of dough' (White, 2021, p. 6). The whole culture is broken. Ezekiel 34 argues that only God can fix it.

These are the accusations against the shepherds. They have been self-serving; namely, abusing their charges to serve themselves. They have exploited their position to provide for themselves while depriving others. The shepherds grow fat while the sheep starve. White comments, 'For those, like myself, who have left a spiritually abusive environment feeling fleeced, drained dry and starved of nourishment, this metaphor paints a painfully accurate picture' (White, 2021, p. 9). The shepherds have also failed to protect the sheep. They show no interest in the health of the flock, nor any concern for those sheep who have wandered off. They are not prepared to invest time or energy in the well-being of others.

> The combination of selfish provision of privilege for themselves with a complete disregard for the welfare of the sheep, all governed by a harsh and dominating attitude, is one showing total rejection of responsibility. This combination appears repeatedly in spiritually abusive environments even today. (White, 2021, p. 9)

The impact is catastrophic. Nowhere is safe. The sheep scatter, vulnerable to further exploitation and abuse. But despair need not be total; for these sheep belong to the Lord. Where the bad shepherds failed, God will act. Amy White compares the bad shepherds and God (White, 2021, p. 12). Her comparison is summarized in Table 2. The bad shepherds and the Lord are opposites. The bad shepherds are rebuked for abusing their privileges and for their aggressive use of power. God will not tolerate this and will step in to end it.

Table 2: Ezekiel 34: comparison between bad shepherds and God

Ezekiel 34.4: the bad shepherds	Ezekiel 34.16: God
The **weak** you have not strengthened, And the **sick** you have not healed, And the **injured** you have not bound up, And the **strayed** you have not brought back And the **lost** you have not searched out	The **lost** *I will* seek, And the **strayed** *I will* bring back, And the **injured** *I will* bind up, And the **weak** *I will* strengthen, And the **fat** and the **strong** *I will* destroy. *I will* shepherd them with justice.

(White, 2021, p. 12)

The flock will also be judged. There are limitations to the shepherd/sheep metaphor, as the 'sheep' may perpetrate abuse. This is particularly conceivable when sheep have relational power or financial influence, a structural vote, or a sense of intellectual or verbal superiority over their leader(s) (White, 2021, p. 14).

The message of the Hebrew Scriptures is that anyone who abuses power will face divine retribution.

Jesus' response to hypocritical religiosity

This section discusses the woes against the Pharisees in Matthew 23 and the clearing of the temple (Matt. 21.12–17; Mark 11.15–19; Luke 19.45–6; John 2.13–22): two examples of Jesus' responses to the misuse of spiritual authority.

FAITH, POWER AND ABUSE: A CHRISTIAN REFLECTION

Matthew 23 is a series of 'woes' against the Pharisees and other religious leaders. The language is harsh. For example, Jesus says:

> Woe to you, scribes and Pharisees, hypocrites! For you tithe mint, dill, and cummin, and have neglected the weightier matters of the law: justice and mercy and faith. It is these you ought to have practised without neglecting the others. You blind guides! You strain out a gnat but swallow a camel! (vv. 23–4)

Before discussing the passage in detail, it is worth recognizing that paying attention to small details is not necessarily a sign someone is a religious hypocrite. Their intention might be to work out what the most righteous and just action is. Is it better, for example, to buy organic fruit and vegetables out of concern for the environment? Or should we buy cheap produce and give the money saved to our church? There is no obvious right answer. Perhaps, the 'rabbis were committed to the belief that it is not a simple matter to say what is "just" and "unjust" in a particular situation' (Hilton and Marshall, 1988, p. 81).

Jesus is clear in Matthew 5.17 that he has not come to destroy the law, but to fulfil it. Notice Jesus does not say tithing herbs is wrong. He says it is one duty among many. Matthew 23 cannot be simply read as teaching that all Pharisees were bad and all Christians are good. But that still leaves us with the challenge of understanding a very aggressive speech from Jesus. Modern Christianity has tended to avoid, rather than deal with, the problem these verses pose:

> Those living in such close historical and emotional proximity to the Holocaust shudder when reading this chapter and ecumenically minded Christians politely avoid these passages. (Overman, 1996, p. 319)

But if we want to confront the reality of spiritual abuse, we must engage with complex and challenging texts. So, what should we make of it?

Jesus' tone is indeed harsh. Perhaps he is condemning religious hypocrisy, when leaders make a big deal of small things while forgetting the more important issues of justice and mercy. These problems are by no means unique to the Pharisees but, rather, 'have their parallels in most religious traditions when the form comes to matter more than the substance' (France, 2007, pp. 854–5). The Church of England case studies make that point very clear.

In Matthew 23.1–12, Jesus warns religious leaders against an inordinate focus on appearance and reputation. This is not just for the Pharisees, but the Disciples as well. Most Christians will have seen excessive deference displayed to people just because of their position or qualifications. This passage is applicable in all times and places, from Jesus' day to today.

Matthew 23.13–36 makes for tough reading. The woes can be understood both as a condemnation of focusing too much on details, while neglecting the main purpose of the law, and as a condemnation of the scribes and Pharisees for failing to recognize that John the Baptist and Jesus were the true messengers of God. Whom do they apply to?

Bible scholar Donald Hagner is at pains to limit the scope of the woes. He argues that they singled out only *some* Pharisees and were part of a debate according to the conventions of the time. Moreover, the debate was focused on whether Jesus or the Pharisees were interpreting the law correctly. It was ultimately a debate about the person of Jesus. Was he just a man? Or something more?

Hagner is clear that the passage is centred on a particular context and has no relevance to the Jews or Judaism of any other time. Moreover, it is a polemic: a negative way of arguing in which you exaggerate the bad points about your opponent to convince your audience that you are right. This means that Matthew 23 cannot even be read as an objective description of what all Pharisees said or believed (Hagner, 1995, pp. 654–5).

In Matthew 23, Jesus respects the role of the scribes and Pharisees as interpreters of the Jewish law. What he is criticizing are the points where he believes their teaching departs from the standards of the law. In particular, he condemns any desire to impress others or any love of prestige or position. These are issues that have an impact on Christians as well; and Jesus warns his followers to watch their own behaviour. This passage is a rebuke designed to keep the followers of Jesus on the straight and narrow.

But that does not hide the shocking nature of some of the text. Matthew 23.13–33 is perhaps the harshest passage in the New Testament (Hagner, 1995, p. 672). When reading it, we should remember that, first, this passage does not describe all Pharisees. Second, the material is gathered in one place by Matthew (the parallels in Luke are much more scattered, which implies that Jesus may have said them at different times). This increases their shock value. Third, although there is no word of grace in this passage, the Pharisees were not excluded from Jesus' invitation. In Hagner's view, the only proper use of this passage today is to criticize neither historical nor contemporary Judaism, but solely as a means of criticizing the Christian Church (Hagner, 1995, pp. 655–73).

This discussion of Matthew 23 shows us a clear distinction between warnings and abuse. Warnings are a necessary part of Christian discipleship. Abuse has no place in any authentic expression of faith. Those who have made mistakes or who are in danger of leading other people astray must be warned, challenged and, if necessary, condemned for their failures. But the main use of this passage is for critical self-reflection. Regular examination of thoughts and actions, potentially guided by a pastoral supervisor, is a necessity for a healthy Christian leadership and culture.

Scholars have discussed Jesus' actions in the Jerusalem temple for a long time. A book on spiritual abuse is not the place to enter the detail of those debates. My focus is on learning from Jesus' actions about when and how to confront spiritually inappropriate behaviour.

Why did Jesus empty the temple of traders? There is no actual evidence of economic exploitation in the temple. Nor was it simply about the inclusion of the Gentiles: creating space for Gentiles to worship was a side benefit of Jesus' actions. Instead, his primary motivation was judgement on how the Jerusalem aristocracy controlled the temple (Keener, 2003, pp. 522–6).

Jesus made space for people to pray. Jesus was not concerned with the fact of money-changing or the sale of suitably pure animals for sacrifice. The problem was the location of these transactions. The rebuke was aimed at the temple authorities for permitting such activities in an inappropriate place. Jesus was confronting and challenging those who controlled the temple (France, 2007, p. 784).

The lesson for confronting spiritual abuse is that we must be ready to tackle powerful elites, who have a strong, vested interest in keeping things as they are. The fact that people of power and influence supported spiritual abusers such as John Smyth, Peter Ball, Mike Pilavachi and Jonathan Fletcher (all discussed in the chapter on the Church of England cases) is highly relevant here. It is not that people were unaware of inappropriate and abusive behaviour; rather, they did not see a need to challenge it.

Jesus took decisive action. He interrupted the arrangements for worshipping God. He clearly had his reasons, could justify his actions and had the means to act (Casey, 1997, p. 311). The point about the disruption of divine worship is important. Think about Catherine Beaumont's example of inappropriate touching during the Peace at a Holy Communion service. In her best-case scenario, the priest would stop the service and deal with the matter, then and there, rather than waiting (Beaumont, 2020, pp. 128–9). Spiritually abusive behaviour cannot be tolerated and so the first opportunity to challenge it must be seized upon, however inappropriate or inconvenient some might regard the action as being.

Spiritually abusive behaviour and practices stop meaningful engagement with worship. Although I am not equating the traders and money-changers with perpetrators of spiritual abuse, it is notable that once the obstruction is removed, there is greater freedom for worship and growth in faith.

Marc Huys makes four observations about Jesus' actions. First, Jesus' uncharacteristically violent action against the money-changers can only be explained as divine anger. Second, Jesus regards the Jewish temple worship of his day as perverted by secularization and commercialism, and in need of divine intervention. Third, because of Jesus' actions, the chief priests and teachers of the law look for a way to kill him and are ultimately successful in this. Fourth, this is not simply an account of destruction but also of rebuilding, including Jesus' allusion to the Resurrection as well as his suggestion that he himself will replace the temple as the means by which people encounter God (Huys, 2010, pp. 153–4).

All four points connect to responses to spiritual abuse. First, spiritually abusive behaviour doubtless angers God. The challenge for us is not to let human emotions dominate or dictate how we respond. There is space for divine retribution, but not for human revenge. The second point is related: the exploitation of individuals for commercial gain could be a form of spiritual abuse, and there are many other forms as well. These require divine intervention; the challenge for us is how to become the agents of divine intervention without being corrupted by human sinfulness. The third point concerns the negative response to those who call out spiritual abuse. As noted on pp. 39 and 131, whistleblowing always involves a cost, such as potentially being rejected by your own community. I am not aware of anybody who has been killed for exposing spiritually abusive practices, but that does not mean such a horrific outcome is impossible. Fourth, dealing with spiritual abuse does not have to be a wholly negative experience. There is room for hope. People can discover a meaningful and rewarding faith as they recover.

In conclusion, here are three points for how to respond to spiritual abuse. First, warnings and challenging language should primarily be internally directed; that is, used as a tool for self-reflection rather than a means of confronting others. Second, inappropriate behaviour and actions should nevertheless be challenged. Third, such challenges will be costly, but the price is worth paying. None of us is Jesus: of course we might get things wrong, but that is no reason not to try.

Paul's polemic in Galatians

Galatians is Paul's angriest letter. His language is harsh at times. In this section, we will read Galatians to get ideas as to how to confront and challenge spiritually inappropriate behaviour. We do not know for certain why Paul wrote Galatians, but the best guess is that the issues are, first, whether you need to follow Jewish rules and customs to follow Jesus; and second, who has the authority to make that decision. Paul's answer is that, no, you do not need to follow Jewish rules, and he has the authority to make that decision. As Nanos (2002) explains, Paul's response

> may be likened to that of a parent who has caught his or her teenager in a compromising turn justified by the powerful urge of acceptance by the youth's peers, the immediacy of this seeming good too strong to resist, the persuasive power of its logic overwhelming. Paul launches not into a cool reasoned case. He has already explained the facts in the past. So Paul turns to rebuke and ridicule by way of ironic dissociation. Such rhetoric is designed to undermine their confidence, to turn seemingly certain realities into certainly real appearances. (p. 320)

Given how worried Paul is about the Galatian Christians, it is perhaps surprising that so much of the letter is his autobiography. Paul's intention is to establish himself as an authoritative figure who has the right to speak into the situation. He does so both by reminding his audience of his close relationship with them (Gal. 4.12–20) and by describing his life story, including his own conversion and subsequent relationship with those in authority in the Jerusalem Church (1.13—2.14).

Paul also describes his own position in relation to the law to show what he wants the audience to do (2.15–21). Paul sets out the common ground he believes he shares both with Barnabas and Peter, as well as with the Galatian Christians. This argument is about how to continue in Christ with the aid of the Holy Spirit. It is not about entry into the community of faith but, rather, about stopping the Galatians leaving it (Witherington, 1998, pp. 171–2). Paul therefore describes appropriate (Gal. 2.19–21) and inappropriate (2.18) courses of action to demonstrate what he thinks they should do.

Paul establishes his authority by describing what he and other people have done. He uses questions to challenge his audience. He uses both rhetorical and more open questions to show the consequences of the position he fears the addressees are adopting. Paul wants to demonstrate the dangers of such a position and so persuade them to change their minds. An example of this technique is found in the challenge at the start of chapter 3. The series of questions he poses have a mixed series of answers.

The first question, 'Who has bewitched you?' (3.1), is probably exaggerated for effect. Paul is not saying that magic was used. The answer is in one sense clear: everyone knows who Paul means. But they may not have thought about their actions in those terms (Betz, 1979, pp. 130–1; Dunn, 1993, p. 151).

The questions that follow all have equally obvious answers: the addressees received the Spirit by believing what they heard (Gal. 3.2); they are not foolish (3.3); they will not end with the flesh (3.3); their experiences (primarily of the Spirit) were not for nothing (3.4); and God gives them his Spirit and works among them because they believe in what they heard (3.5). Paul uses these questions to tell the audience they do not need to follow Jewish laws to follow Jesus.

Paul also gives some instructions for how to live out life in the Spirit. Four times Paul describes something and then gives an instruction that flows logically from the statement.

1 Abraham's belief in God before he was circumcised means the addressees should know they are descendants of Abraham (3.6–7).
2 They should imitate Paul's example: 'become as I am, for I also have become as you are' (4.12).
3 They have been freed, therefore, to stand firm and should not become slaves (5.1).
4 They 'were called to freedom'; therefore they should not 'use [their] freedom as an opportunity for self-indulgence' but serve one another in love (5.13).

Paul gives direct instructions seven times. All bar one (4.21) are in the concluding ethical instructions (5.13—6.10); they are used to give commands for how to live in harmony with others (5.15, 16), to care for others (6.1, 2, 6) and to watch one's personal spirituality (6.4, 7). Paul blends description with instruction.

For example, the statement 'If you let yourselves be circumcised, Christ is of no advantage to you' (5.2) is effectively an instruction not to be circumcised.

In conclusion, Paul's strategy in Galatians is to mix description, questions and instruction. He is mounting a strong challenge to the addressees and setting out, in no uncertain terms, the course of action he expects them to pursue.

Paul's strategy in how he wrote his letter to the Galatians gives a framework for responding to spiritual abuse. Those new to the faith are particularly vulnerable to exploitation. Regular, open, engaging teaching and training are required. Inappropriate behaviour must be challenged, initially in private but then, if this is unsuccessful, in public. Those bringing the challenge must establish their authority and credentials for doing so and must be recognized by those in the Church. Questions are a powerful tool ('Is it appropriate for a leader to wrestle with interns dressed only in their underwear?'), especially if the answer is clear. Instructions flowing from descriptions are useful. ('He was alone in his bedroom with a teenage boy. Never do this.') Direct instructions are important tools for equipping congregations to respond to the risks of abuse. ('Challenge behaviour if you think it is wrong.') The reviews of the different Church of England case studies discussed in Chapter 5 left little in doubt as to the course of action the reviewers expected. This fits with Paul's own strategy in writing to the Church in Galatia. If something is wrong, it will not do to leave it unchallenged.

How do we lead?

In this chapter, I have reflected theologically on spiritual abuse. After two words of warning, I discussed connections between biblical teaching and the theory of agency and education. The main insight concerning agency was that individuals are held accountable for their decisions and actions and will face the judgement of God. At the same time, however, God is at work within them to enable them to face judgement with the confidence that, in Christ, all things are forgiven. Leaders are

FAITH, POWER AND ABUSE: A CHRISTIAN REFLECTION

accountable but can have confidence in Christ. I reflected briefly on education (noting the warning about teachers facing a stricter judgement), with an emphasis on education in the home and of an open-ended, creative approach to teaching. Leaders should be both creative teachers and diligent students.

Turning to the Hebrew Scriptures, I considered four texts: Leviticus 10, Ezekiel 34, Amos 5 and Jeremiah 36. In these passages, individuals and groups, especially groups of leaders, are rebuked and held accountable for their actions. All those who abuse the responsibilities they have been given will be judged by God. Ezekiel 34 was used by Amy White to develop a theological definition of spiritual abuse. Her insights are particularly valuable in the ongoing discussion. Leaders should reflect on how they use power.

When discussing the teaching and actions of Jesus, I considered Matthew 23. The harsh language and warnings against the Pharisees should primarily be used as a tool for self-reflection, rather than as a means of judging other people. Jesus' actions in the temple, where he challenged the religious leaders, were also considered. The implication for responding to spiritual abuse is for us to try to become channels of righteous anger against abuse and to respond robustly, while recognizing the potential personal cost of speaking out.

Finally, I explored Paul's concern for the Galatian Christians. He wrote to warn them of the risk they faced in adding unnecessary requirements to their belief in Christ as saviour. This is a stark warning for any who perpetrate spiritual abuse, whether wittingly or unwittingly, as they are stepping outside the bounds of what is acceptable in Christianity. Do we ask people to do things that are unnecessary additions to faith in Jesus?

I conclude with two final observations. The first is that when Jesus sent out both the Twelve and the Seventy-Two, he sent them out in pairs. The Church of England case studies were all about unaccountable individuals. If they had ministered with others, who were empowered to correct and rebuke them as necessary, would they have perpetrated abuse?

Second, we should learn from Paul's insights in 2 Corinthians 12:

SAFER FAITHS, SAFER FOLLOWERS

To keep me from being too elated, a thorn was given to me in the flesh, a messenger of Satan to torment me, to keep me from being too elated. Three times I appealed to the Lord about this, that it would leave me, but he said to me, 'My grace is sufficient for you, for power is made perfect in weakness'. So, I will boast all the more gladly of my weaknesses, so that the power of Christ may dwell in me. (vv. 7–9)

It is when we admit our vulnerability and weakness that we are best equipped to serve Christ, and least at risk of abusing others.

PART IV

Next Steps

In this book, I have discussed spiritual abuse in detail, relying on both theoretical insights and the experiences of 27 different people. This is a relatively small number; but it is big enough to provide a robust framework for theoretical and practical reflection. In this final part, I offer some useful ideas as to how to respond best to the risk and reality of spiritual abuse.

There are three chapters. Chapter 7 has suggestions for how to work with the authorities. Trust between faith groups and authorities such as the police can be tricky. This chapter looks at the challenges and solutions for working together to prevent spiritual abuse and protect those at risk. Chapter 8 contains ideas for an awareness-raising workshop, including scenarios to discuss. It is full of practicable ideas for awareness sessions, complete with real-life scenarios to help people think through difficult situations and recognize warning signs in their own communities. Chapter 9 includes three sample sermons for Safeguarding Sunday (usually, the third Sunday in November; see https://safeguardingsunday.org). These offer insights from Scripture on protecting the vulnerable and creating safe spaces for worship.

7

Working with the Authorities

Mr Pilavachi and Bishop David Pytches (who was then the Vicar of St Andrew's, Chorleywood) were aware that Matt had been sexually abused at least a year before the police became involved. We have corroborated information that Matt told Mr Pilavachi about the abuse, which was then referred by Mr Pilavachi to Bishop Pytches. Instead of calling the police or social services, Bishop Pytches then organised a meeting with Matt's mother and stepfather where this was disclosed. (Scolding and Fullbrook, 2024, p. 41)

Distrust of, or uncertainty about, engaging with the authorities (the police and social services) kept coming up as I talked with people about spiritual abuse. They recognized that the police and social services have a role to play in protecting individuals at risk and ensuring perpetrators are brought to justice. But they were also worried about the way in which the authorities might address these pressing problems. In one of the focus groups, someone talked about the gap between the authorities and faith groups. The point was made that sometimes a concern is passed from a faith group to the police or social services but will often get passed back because, from the perspective of the police or social services, it does not cross the statutory threshold. That is, the situation is not thought to be serious enough for the police or social services to get involved. But the faith group knows that something has gone wrong and needs help to deal with the problem. The required response must be agile and informed, requiring close working founded on mutual understanding and trust. I use the St Philip's Centre's four values of encounter, understanding, trust and cooperation to explore how best to bridge the gap that exists between religious groups and the authorities.

Encounter

Within the St Philip's Centre framework, encounters should be meaningful and sustained: they should be an opportunity to talk with somebody whose life experience and values are very different from your own. An encounter should be honest and open-minded, without one person being more powerful than others. People should be free to say what they really think, within appropriate boundaries. Are the authorities equipped to do this? At least two participants thought they were not. One person, who had suffered spiritual abuse, commented: 'From my experience, most of the professionals that I have gone to, both privately and otherwise, very few of them could actually help me in my distressed state.'

Another participant suggested:

> I don't think even the authorities feel capable to help because, from what we've seen, particularly in sort of religious issues [in Leicester] over the past couple of years, they're pretty incompetent, aren't they? And the people above don't seem to understand.

Another participant proposed that there is a role for the police in educating people of faith around their rights and the potential police responses to abusive practices. Is it the case that the authorities do not understand? Is it that they lack the resources and/or legal powers to act in the way religious institutions want them to?

If these are the problems, what can be done? At the St Philip's Centre, we base a lot of our work on Allport's contact theory, which, at its simplest, is a belief that intergroup acceptance and cooperation is promoted when people spend time with one another. It is a reasonably logical and common-sense hypothesis: namely, that if you get to know a person as a person, you are far less likely to feel prejudiced against them. In my experience, it works about 90 to 95 per cent of the time. In most encounters with people who see the world differently from one another, participants leave with a greater appreciation of how the other person views life. Occasionally, something goes wrong and prejudice is reinforced or, as one participant experienced, help and support that are sought are not provided. Then you must work all the harder to undo the damage that has inadvertently been done.

Allport formalized his theory to argue that intergroup acceptance and cooperation are best provided under four conditions:

1 if everyone has equal status
2 if members of the group hold common goals
3 if there is cooperation within the group
4 if there is support from or by authorities.

Equal status does not mean that everybody comes into the group with equal prestige. Rather, it means that every member's knowledge, skills and opinions are regarded as equally important. It also means that every person in the encounter feels that their contributions are regarded as equal with those of everybody else; and everybody is working together towards common goals. Prejudice within groups is reduced by actively involving all members in a shared task or goal. No one member is more important than anybody else in achieving that goal. Everybody must feel safe to speak and to take the lead, as appropriate. If a group is officially recognized by the leaders of an organization, then there is greater acceptance of their need to exist and function (Gierman-Riblon and Salloway, 2013, pp. 59–60).

Allport's theory can be summarized as shown in Table 3.

All of this sounds very good in theory, but does it work in practice? Thomas Pettigrew and Linda Tropp examined hundreds of studies of contact theory, and they concluded that contact does reduce prejudice (Pettigrew and Tropp, 2006). When people encounter those who see the world differently from themselves, invariably their prejudices are reduced and their willingness to engage with differences increased. And the positive effect ripples out beyond participants in the immediate contact situation. An encounter between a police officer and a survivor of spiritual abuse does not just mean that the police officer understands the survivor and vice versa. It means that the police officer is better

Table 3: A summary of Allport's contact theory

Condition	Meaning	Example
Equal status	Members of the contact situation should not have an unequal, hierarchical relationship.	Members should not have an employer/employee or instructor/student relationship.
Cooperation	Members should work together in a non-competitive environment.	Students working together in a group project.
Common goals	Members must rely on each other to achieve their shared desired goal.	Members of a sports team.
Support by social and institutional authorities	There should not be social or institutional authorities that explicitly or implicitly punish contact, and there should be authorities that support positive contact.	There should not be official laws enforcing segregation.

(Everett, 2013, p. 2)

equipped to engage with other survivors; the survivor also has a clearer understanding of the limitations of police powers.

Must all Allport's conditions be in place to achieve a positive outcome? Happily not. Even when all Allport's key conditions are not met, studies still show significant relationships between contact and the reduction in prejudice. Allport's conditions are helpful but not necessary for producing positive contact outcomes. They are 'facilitating conditions that enhance the tendency for positive contact outcomes to emerge' rather than being essential for change to take place (Pettigrew and Tropp, 2006, p. 766).

It is also the case that short- and long-term contact does not always reduce prejudice. Jeffrey Denis conducted research in a small town in a remote area of Canada. He concluded that, although white and indigenous Canadians broadly had good relationships, they still displayed what he terms 'laissez-faire racism' and other forms of prejudice. People did not always generalize beyond their individual experience of those who were different from themselves. For example, just because they got on with somebody did not mean to say that everybody was equally likable. A white Canadian might like, or even be married to, an individual indigenous Canadian, but that did not mean the white Canadian was no longer prejudiced against the indigenous population (Denis, 2015).

While the limitations of contact must be recognized, it is nevertheless the case that more meaningful and sustained encounters between the authorities and those who have experienced spiritual abuse can only have a positive impact on dealing with the problem. This is because all those involved will develop a better understanding of the issues and what can be done in response.

Understanding

The St Philip's Centre's second value is understanding. Understanding does not mean agreement. Any encounter that engages with the realities of spiritual abuse will include disagreement as those involved in the conversation compare their world-views. As one participant explained:

> I also want to say that I actually think any abuse has a spiritual component because we are spiritual beings. But I'm conscious, in a secular world, not everybody would understand what I was talking about.

Another participant asked, 'What will happen if those who do not understand faith seek to enforce a law on spiritual abuse?' Lack of understanding could potentially have serious consequences.

Staff at the St Philip's Centre regularly run religious literacy training for people at a variety of ages and life stages, from school children to police officers and social workers. Mutual incomprehension sometimes features as religious and non-religious world-views meet. This can be a feature of discussions about spiritual abuse. A different participant argued that spiritual abuse is not a useful category primarily because it is difficult or even impossible for the authorities to measure and report accurately.

Similarly, in a focus group, it was questioned whether a case of purely spiritual abuse would ever lead to a criminal conviction. Would the jury understand the issues? As one participant said, it is very, very easy to minimize any kind of psychological or emotional abuse. When a survivor of abuse is telling their story, they are often recounting many instances over a long time. Any one of those on their own might not seem that great: 'So, it's very easy to shut somebody down very early on in what they are trying to share.'

Therefore, as another participant explained, staff in the police and social services need to become more knowledgeable about the forms of abuse and the forms of toxicity. Yet another participant argued the authorities would be helpful, if 'they're trained. They might be fearful over their lack of knowledge or worry about being accused of being racist or anti-religion or whatever.'

But what should the training include? It is not enough to know what happened. Motivation and world-view must be explored, and differences acknowledged. One participant said:

> I think my fear would be the authorities see faith, I mean, think faith is belief in God, and belief in God looks like this, this and this, and therefore you know this is what abuse of that would look like. And I think it's too complex. And I think it's too personal.

A different participant made a similar point about culture:

I think in our setting in particular, there is always a fear that is not just the spiritual aspect, but not understanding the cultural backgrounds of most of the people who have come here, for instance, spanking a child is considered appropriate or normal within most African cultures.

Understanding someone's world-view does not mean you agree that it is correct. It is perfectly possible for a police officer or social worker to believe it is wrong to spank a child but nevertheless seek to understand why a father of Nigerian heritage might believe it to be acceptable. For it is only once this individual's culture and world-view are understood that the police officer or social worker can develop an appropriate response. Equally, faith-based organizations have work to do in understanding the culture and demands placed on the authorities. And we must all be aware of how swiftly culture has changed. I was smacked on the bottom by my primary school head teacher, in front of the whole school. That was less than 40 years ago – but such an act would be unthinkable now. It takes time to develop a deep understanding, which will also result in the development of trust.

Trust

Understanding is insufficient for establishing a productive working relationship between the authorities and faith-based organizations. Trust is also required. I understand trust to be the confidence, based on experience over time, that you not only have my best interests at heart but you will also act in accordance with my needs, even if that is personally costly and difficult for you and possibly for me. Trust is more than arms-length tolerance; it is deeper than respect based on competence. Trust presumes a profound sharing from the heart, in conditions of safety and security.

One of the focus groups discussed the cost of speaking out, arguing that whistleblowing is always costly and always resisted. As one participant put it: 'An investigation is brutal; and no matter how sensitively it is done, I would question whether anything can ever be confidential or is ever kept truly confidential.' People do not come forward to share their experiences of spiritual abuse with the authorities because they do not trust that they will be looked after or that the case will be taken seriously.

Trust is earned over time and at a cost. I believe there is a Dutch proverb that says, 'Trust arrives on foot but leaves on horseback.' This presents a challenge for relationships between religious groups and the authorities; staff in the latter organizations often move on after periods of time that religious groups regard as far too short for establishing trust. It can take decades to establish the deep trust that is required for people to share their experiences of abuse.

Perhaps the place to begin is working with those who inadvertently abuse; this requires some trust, but not as much as is needed for victims of spiritual abuse to come forward. A participant asked about the provision of a safe space for critical self-reflection. The space must be psychologically safe enough to enable people to speak out about concerns they may have and what they need to put into place to ensure that they do not end up harming others or themselves. But what is psychological safety?

> Psychological safety describes a belief that neither the formal nor informal consequences of interpersonal risks, like asking for help or admitting failure, will be punitive. (Edmondson, 2019, p. 15)

Psychological safety is not about being nice; nor is it a personality trait; and it is not about lowering performance standards. Creating a psychologically safe organization requires three steps. First, invite participation, not simply by saying, 'My door is open', but by going out and actively seeking the views of others, with questions such as 'Is everything in our practice as safe as it should be?' Second, respond when people speak up. There is no point in asking if you have no intention of acting on what you hear. Thank people for speaking up and explain what will happen next. And make sure you act. Third, make it safe for some kinds of failure: not in the sense of preventable mistakes (such as failure to keep accurate records) or complex failures, which result from unique and novel combinations of events and actions that give rise to unwanted outcomes. But if a failure comes from an experiment that went wrong, that should not be punished as it can provide an opportunity for learning.

A framework of trust could be established if religious groups and the authorities work together to help religious leaders reflect on what constitutes healthy practice and how the authorities can assist in setting appropriate boundaries. Returning to the example of whether it is right or wrong to spank a child, a culturally sensitive approach by social services would enable religious leaders to develop sufficient trust to share more complex concerns. Psychological safety must be in place if we are to establish trust. It is a necessary staging post for developing true cooperation. The authorities and religious organizations must establish psychologically safe relationships as a foundation for the trust that is required when responding to spiritual abuse.

Trust develops slowly and gradually. It is as important for the authorities to develop trust in religious institutions as it is for religious institutions to trust the authorities. The first stage is to work with the willing on more straightforward issues. When trust is deepened through successful completion of these tasks, there is potential for cooperation on more complicated challenges. Cooperation is therefore the fruit of well-watered and carefully nurtured mutual trust.

Cooperation

One participant argued that the authorities have a role to prevent all responses to spiritual abuse from remaining internal matters within a faith-based organization or religious community. They added that there remains an issue of timing and training, to ensure that interventions are appropriate and will contribute towards resolving the issues, not making them worse.

A second participant agreed with this suggestion. They argued that education about risks must necessarily go hand in hand with the possibility of consequences if appropriate practices and healthy cultures remained undeveloped.

Cooperation is not cuddly. It is concrete, specific, proportionate and timely. It requires tough decisions and decisive action built on established foundations of understanding and trust.

We must work together

Spiritual abuse is not a problem that an individual or, indeed, a single group of individuals can tackle. Systematic failures require a system-wide response. The aim of this reflection has been to begin bridging the gap that exists between religious groups and statutory authorities. Both need to encounter each other in meaningful and sustained ways to develop an understanding about their cultures and how they work. These encounters could be modelled on tried-and-tested training courses run by the St Philip's Centre, which combine theoretical, scene-setting and thought-provoking input with interaction between the authorities and religious leaders. Mutual understanding can lead to the development of trust that forms the basis of cooperation to tackle serious incidents of spiritual abuse.

8

Raising Awareness in Your Community

Something was not okay, and I share the responsibility of having allowed it to happen. (Mullen, 2020, p. xv)

I have two principles that I use to guide and shape any awareness-raising sessions I run in relation to spiritual abuse. The first principle is that the journey is the destination. The point is to have the discussion, not necessarily to reach a firm conclusion. By raising the awareness that my behaviour may be unhealthy or even abusive, I am alert to the risk, develop greater agency and I am far less likely to do something inappropriate.

My second principle is to focus on my own community's issues and not to point fingers at others. There are plenty of examples of spiritually abusive practices within Church of England Christianity. I use these to begin discussions about the problems facing people of many different religions. If I engage in aggressive or confrontational behaviour, we will not arrive at solutions. But if I admit that my denomination has issues, this gives others permission to do the same.

This chapter has two main sections: practical ideas for sessions on raising awareness of spiritual abuse and scenarios to discuss. There are three groups of scenarios: cases of spiritual abuse in general; the abuse of volunteers; and the abuse of employees. The second and third groups may, or may not, be examples of spiritual abuse; the situations may be simply unhelpful or unhealthy. They are included to help you to reflect further on Professor Oakley's continuum of behaviour (see pp. 17–18).

Practical ideas for awareness-raising sessions

Spiritual abuse is an emotive and challenging subject, which might be triggering for those we are working with. We must therefore ensure people are warned, provided with appropriate support and signposted to other agencies as necessary. I often recommend Action on Spiritual Abuse (formerly Replenished Life; https://www.actiononspiritualabuse.org.uk) and Safe Spaces England and Wales (https://www.safespacesenglandandwales.org.uk). For Muslims, there is the US website In Shaykh's Clothing (https://inshaykhsclothing.com). It is also important to develop safe ways of working together, with appropriate boundaries and group commitments. In what follows, I set out some ideas of elements to use in a workshop aimed at raising awareness of the risks and realities of spiritual abuse.

The logical place to start is to develop a working definition of spiritual abuse. I tend to do this by using handouts that give several definitions. Participants work in small groups to critique a definition and develop one of their own. Plenary discussion can follow, with a focus on feeding forward into the next element of the workshop.

If this seems too heavy as a starting point, you could begin by asking people to 'free write' about their understanding of the term 'spiritual'. Free writing is a creative technique where you write for five minutes without worrying about spelling or grammar. No one sees what you have written, but people are invited to share anything they want. Once you have a group understanding of 'spiritual', you could then reflect on what abuse might look like. You do not have to use the word 'abuse'. You might ask, 'What would get in the way of your being spiritual?'

It is important to acknowledge the fact that sometimes spiritual abuse happens to people gradually; they can be like the proverbial frog floating in a saucepan of increasingly hot water. This makes recognizing and defining spiritual abuse even more difficult. The first conversation seems harmless, but the final one is clearly dangerous. There are also questions of intention. Sometimes an individual may deliberately use their position of spiritual power to abuse others. But it is also possible that the abuse may be unthinking or unintentional, as the individual concerned lacks the self-awareness to realize the impact of their words or actions. When and how is the line crossed into an abusive relationship? I am not a legal expert; nor is this book designed to provide legally watertight advice as to what is or is not spiritual abuse. Rather, the aim is that through discussing different scenarios, you will have a better sense of what abusive behaviour is; that way you can develop practical steps to take to ensure that it does not have an impact on your faith community. This will protect the individuals within your community, as well as the reputation of your community as a whole and its relationship with the wider public.

This is the stage to introduce Professor Oakley's continuum and the associated examples. At this point, I might ask participants to work in pairs or threes to decide where to place one-line scenarios on the continuum of 'healthy', 'unhelpful', 'unhealthy' and 'spiritual abuse'. Alternatively, you could print out each of the four stages of the continuum and stick them up around the room. People could stand next to the one they think is most apposite. Examples of one-line scenarios include

- publicly rebuking an adult who has not memorized a Scripture verse;
- giving sweets to a child who has memorized Scripture;
- telling a teenager that they can be friends only with people of their religion and gender;
- telling a 12-year-old off for using WhatsApp during a worship service;
- expecting a mentee to report which films they are watching;
- publicly praising a generous donor;
- admitting personal struggles with anger management in a sermon;
- publicly sharing someone's personal medical details so people know how to pray for them;
- putting photos of people taken during a service on your personal social media account;
- buying copies of a book on spiritual disciplines and giving them to people who you think would benefit from reading one.

Many of these actions could potentially be positive and healthy. Some cultures celebrate generous gifts publicly, in part to reduce the risk of the private misuse of funds. If someone asks to be held accountable for which films they watch, then asking them regularly is entirely appropriate. Sharing photos with consent is fine; without consent, doing so may breach data protection laws. A 12-year-old should not be on WhatsApp, as the minimum age is 13; a warning to stop using social media may be entirely positive. Appropriate sharing in sermons is healthy, but it is possible to overshare or, as I heard someone put it, the preacher can metaphorically 'bleed all over the congregation'.

The purpose of the exercise is to encourage discussion and personal reflection. Why, for example, do some Christians bribe children with sweets to encourage them to take part in an all-age service? The topic could be approached through quiet individual reflection or small group discussion. You could use apps such as slido (https://www.slido.com) or Mentimeter (https://www.mentimeter.com) as interactive and anonymous ways of gathering questions or insights. People can then vote with sticky dots as to which is the best description. Alternatively, you could use a 'human rainbow'. Designate one side of the room as 'healthy' and the opposite side as 'spiritual abuse'. Give a one-line scenario and ask people to stand where they think is most appropriate along the rainbow. You can then ask people to say why they have picked their chosen place to stand.

You might also want to use 'projective methods'. Participants are given a question or theme: for example, a question such as 'How do I feel about spiritual abuse?' or topics such as 'the impact of abuse', 'agency' or 'confidence in dealing with abuse'. Participants can then be invited to pick a picture or an object from a range of alternatives and discuss their choices, either in groups or in a plenary session. The aim here is to help participants articulate thoughts and feelings they might initially struggle to put into words. If you have time, you could 'map' complex relationships using buttons, figures or objects.

Participants could be invited to bring to the group a scriptural text, a song, a hymn or a poem that speaks to them either of the realities and impact of spiritual abuse, or of developing agency or shaping a suitable response. This could be journalled by individuals, or discussed in pairs or in a plenary session. The participants might write poetry, draw or paint as a response. People could take photographs and explain their choices to the group. If appropriate, there might be corporate worship or prayer.

If you have a suitably qualified facilitator, you could use reflective exercises. For example, you could lead a meditation on what a spiritually fulfilling place looks like. In an exercise of this type, people can sit quietly, with their eyes closed, or walk around if they prefer. The person leading the meditation invites everyone to imagine a spiritually fulfilling place, gradually building up detail. At some point, a disruptive element is introduced, which gets in the way for a while, but subsequently leaves. It is important for participants to feel safe and comfortable, both during the meditation and afterwards, as you reflect on what you have learned by taking part.

There are lots of ways of raising awareness about spiritual abuse. The key point is that the session must be both safe and have sound boundaries, and be appropriately charged, as Parker Palmer puts it (see p. 61). Survivor testimony can be included, if suitable, or you could discuss scenarios. In the next few sections, I have given some examples.

Scenarios of spiritual abuse

In this section, there are 11 scenarios of a situation that may, or may not, be spiritual abuse. They are a mixture of anonymized real cases and fictional possibilities. They are included because, in my experience, discussing scenarios is one of the best ways of helping you to think about what presents a safeguarding concern and what does not. All the scenarios have been checked for plausibility with members of the religious community that is referenced. The scenarios are deliberately short and lacking detail; their purpose is to stimulate discussion rather than to present a problem to be solved.

The scenarios could stimulate personal reflection, journalling, prayer, poetry or drawing. They could be discussed in groups, used in conjunction with the creative methods discussed above or examined in a plenary session.

As you read a scenario, ask yourself these questions:

- What is the experience and motivation of the victim?
- What is the experience and motivation of the perpetrator?
- What would this look like to an outsider?
- What should be done to respond?

These questions should help you to develop your own understanding of what constitutes spiritual abuse.

Scenario 1: Sue

Sue, 67, has been in and out of psychiatric hospitals for almost 25 years, following a breakdown she had in her early 40s. At a London hospital, she had made good progress as an inpatient. Shortly before she was expecting to be discharged, she claims she was subjected to an exorcism by an agency doctor, who was originally from Nigeria.

According to her account, the doctor led her into a consultation room and closed the blinds. Sue said:

> She then leaned over the table and grabbed my hands and held me across the table, totally imprisoning me. She was so strong that I couldn't wriggle out of her grip. She didn't speak to me and never looked at me. She then started chanting and praying in a language I had never heard. I was crying and sobbing and begging her to let me go. I was terrified. I felt acute, animal terror.

After the incident, Sue said her recovery went into reverse. She added, 'I feel seriously traumatized. I feel very unsafe in the world.'

Scenario 2: Melanie

Melanie was experiencing difficulties in her personal life – she had an abusive husband and a daughter who had been diagnosed as autistic – when her vicar and others in the leadership of her Anglican church suggested that she needed deliverance.

One day, Melanie fainted during a choir rehearsal.

> As I was regaining consciousness, they said that I looked at them with an inhuman face and laughed at them. I was told this was a mocking spirit. Rather than get medical attention or first aid, they took me for prayers and kept me there in quite a forceful manner for three hours, despite my being in considerable pain. Later, it was discovered that I had a perforated eardrum, and that had been the cause of the faint.

A few months afterwards, she was collected from her home and taken to the house of a person unknown to her.

> Things took a really strange turn. They pushed me to my knees and shouted in my face, saying the spirits were in me and that I was going to bring down the church. They forced me to be sick. It went on for about two hours. I felt very traumatized and just blanked it out. They said I mustn't tell anyone about it, and I mustn't come to church for six months until they were sure all the demons were gone. I was in a state of shock.

Later, one of those involved suggested to Melanie that her four-year-old daughter might not be autistic, but possessed by demons, and that the child needed deliverance.

Scenario 3: Aysha

Aysha is nine years old. Her family are devout Muslims and insist that she covers her hair whenever she goes outside. She is not permitted to speak to any men, except for her father and brothers. She is expected to fast during the month of Ramadan and to attend two hours of supplementary school each weekday.

Aysha is not allowed to listen to pop music or watch television; she must spend her free time helping her mother with household chores. Aysha attends an Islamic school for girls, where the curriculum is focused on rote learning of the Qur'an and traditions about the Prophet Muhammad.

Aysha has recently discovered Facebook and has set up her own account on the tablet her parents bought her to help her memorize the Qur'an. Sometimes when she is in her bedroom, supposedly practising her Qur'anic recitations, she spends her time on Facebook instead. She has recently become Facebook friends with Abdullah, who introduced himself as a 15-year-old *hafiz* (someone who has memorized the entire Qur'an). He has offered to help Aysha and wants to set up a video chat with her. Aysha does not know what to do.

Scenario 4: Sheila

Sheila is a 26-year-old ultra-Orthodox Jewish woman, with one small child. She said that four weeks into dating Levi, they had got engaged. Then something happened that left her worried and confused. She said:

> He overreacted to something that was just – it was some kind of mistake or something. And he wouldn't believe that it wasn't anything to get worked up about. I just thought it was weird. His response was – I can't remember, to be honest. Maybe he called me. He didn't say, 'I'm very sorry I overreacted. It's because I had this bad experience before or whatever.' He didn't say anything like that. So, I said to him, 'I'm upset. I don't think this is going to work, goodbye.'

Sheila went on to explain:

> I then got a phone call a day later or that day – I think it was that day – from his rabbi. He was at yeshiva at the time. The rabbi told me I was lucky to have this match, that he was very excellent; and that it is the God-given responsibility for a wife to respect her husband and to serve as his helper in managing

their household and nurturing the next generation. The rabbi said I should stop being oversensitive and allow my husband to protect, provide for and lead the family I was to become part of. So, I let it slide. It was the beginning of me thinking that I am just too sensitive. The rabbi said that I had accepted the match and, now I was engaged, I had to continue with the marriage, despite Levi's negative traits. In my heart, I knew that if I walked away, I would lose the support of many of my friends in the community, and I just couldn't face being that alone.

Scenario 5: James

James is 15. He explains:

I met the vicar at his home at first, in the living room. He told me that we could do without the formal mentoring book and instructions because he wanted to be more friends than mentor/mentee. He told me that the mentoring should increase to every other Tuesday. We met in the living room for a couple of times, but he then suggested that the room was not suitable because it was too public. If we wanted to share things, we ought to go to the bedroom. The meetings in the bedroom lasted two hours or so. During the meetings, we studied the Bible and prayed for each other. During prayer, we laid hands on each other's head, shoulders, chest and back. We also played a 'trust' game whereby one of us would fall backwards to be caught by the other.

The contact grew further until it was daily contact, studying the Bible, praying for each other for up to one and a half hours per day. I found this too intense, but I found it impossible to tell him that I wanted less contact. The vicar became angry if I did not ring him or respond to his texts, and he would say that this is not what friends did. At times, the vicar was in tears in front of me. He would be angry if I did not come to an evening service because of being with my girlfriend. He made it clear that the relationship was getting in the way of the mentoring.

Then, in March, the vicar moved in with my family. My mother worked at the church and was a new member of the congregation. She welcomed the opportunity to support the vicar, whom she believed to be lonely and unwell. Once he had moved in, the daily phone calls stopped. However, the pressure remained intense. He came on holiday with the family to Crete in July.

Other members of the church raised concerns about the intensity of the contact between me and the vicar, which led to the involvement of the bishop. He moved out of the family home in September. Me and Mum were very angry at other members of the church making these complaints and bringing this situation about.

Scenario 6: Timothy

From the outside looking in, it looked like the perfect life. I grew up in London and on a boat in the Bahamas, with my parents and twin brother, but I always felt empty inside and sad. I didn't really fit in. Most of my family died before I was 15, and then my father died. I was always seeking for what happens after we die: why are we here?

When I was 33, I wandered into a tantric Buddhist meditation seminar, and I sat down to meditate. I was expecting an older woman, with long grey hair, a white robe and spa music. Instead, it was a young woman wearing what looked like an Armani business suit and stiletto heels. She put on techno music and said, 'Let's meditate', and put on her sunglasses. I closed my eyes to meditate and had this incredible experience. Everything goes white and there's so much peace. I realized this was what I had been searching for my entire life. I thought, 'I don't care who this woman is. I don't care what she says. I'm home.'

I now feel incredibly fulfilled, like my life suddenly has a purpose. I no longer feel empty or sad. I am going to the meditation classes every week, and they are the highlight of my week. But recently, one of the leaders suggested that I also begin going to his house for one-to-one meditation sessions, to help me improve and grow more quickly. I want to, but I am also uncomfortable spending that much time alone with that particular teacher.

Scenario 7: Tara

I was doing my PhD in consciousness and spirituality. I went to a talk and there was a Hindu guru talking very eloquently about consciousness and the mind, so I started training with him. Before I knew it, I was completely hooked. Then he said: 'I can't teach you any more. You need to go to my guru in India, who's absolutely enlightened. This is your chance.'

After three days at the ashram in India, I'd eaten lunch and I remember slowly, slowly trying to hang onto the wall, and my fingernails scratching the wall, slipping down and losing consciousness. The next thing I knew, I was in the room they had given me, and he was on top of me. I didn't get out of that room for three months.

The thing that confused me when I came home is that I couldn't explain to people what had happened. He'd be on top of me, I'd freeze, disassociate, and an hour or two later I'd be sitting there thinking: 'This is not what I came here for. I thought he was supposed to have my best interests at heart.'

Then he'd accuse me of not behaving properly. You wouldn't believe the mind tricks they play. He'd say: 'It's because of your Catholic upbringing that you don't like this.'

What people don't understand is when you sit in front of a man or woman with all the pomp and all the incense ... and they say you need to be more loving and kinder and do these prayers and help all sentient beings, you feel your heart open. You feel: 'Yes, I want to be that pure person, I am so grateful to you.' That very pure, open feeling is actually all your own doing, but you think this guru has done something to you.

Scenario 8: Abdul

I grew up as a devout member of the Tablighi Jamaat (TJ) movement, a socially and theologically conservative expression of Islam. I ran away from home in order to train at their madrasa in Dewsbury to be an imam, much to my parents' distress. During my training, I became engaged. Initially, I thought that the senior imams in TJ would approve of this relationship; but they told me I had to break off the engagement or I would go to hell. I did not do so. For many days, including my wedding day, I spent hours praying, asking Allah to spare me from hell.

I lied to my father-in-law, telling him that the leaders of TJ approved of my marriage, but he found out the truth. The leaders of TJ sent me to America to work in a madrasa there as a teacher, where I was paid just $50 per month. They controlled my every movement and eventually it became too much for me. I returned to the UK and tried to leave TJ. This caused me great emotional and psychological distress, and I have been referred to counselling as a result.

I tried to resolve the issue with the leaders of the madrasa in Dewsbury; but they just laughed at me. I do not want to leave Islam; but nor do I want to be part of an organization that has caused me so much pain.

Scenario 9: Funmi

When Funmi was sent to the UK from Nigeria to live with her aunt and uncle at the age of eight, her family thought she was heading for a better life. But living in London soon became a nightmare for Funmi when she was accused of being possessed by evil spirits and causing her mother's death.

Funmi said:

My mum was ill for a long time and became sick and died. I was one of seven children and was sent to England to live with my mum's brother and his wife. My aunt had not been feeling well and was having terrible dreams. She spoke to the pastor in the church the family attended, and he told her someone in the house was doing these things to her. The blame was put on me and I was told I was responsible for everything bad that happened. My aunt and uncle had a baby, and if it cried at night, I was told that was my fault and I was accused of flying during the night. The pastor told me I was the cause of my mum dying and that was a painful moment and as a child, that really affects you.

The pastor tried to organize for Funmi to be returned to Nigeria for exorcism, but the school became aware of the plans, and contacted social services, who intervened to protect her.

Scenario 10: *Savita*

Savita is 14; her parents have told her that they have arranged for her to marry Anil. Anil is three years older than she is, so the marriage will not take place until Savita is 18. But in order to follow their cultural traditions, Savita's parents have made plans for an engagement ceremony to take place in a few months. Savita doesn't want to disobey her parents but, at the same time, there is a boy in her class whom she fancies and had hoped she could start a relationship with. Unsure of what to do, she asked the teacher of her Gujarati class, whom she had always trusted and looked to as a role model, for advice. The teacher went straight to her parents, who were incredibly angry with Savita.

Everything has changed since Savita spoke to her Gujarati teacher. Her parents have told her that it is her family duty to marry the man they have chosen for her. If she disobeys, it will be a disgrace to her family and make it harder for her siblings to find suitable partners. She is still expected to go to school but must come straight home. She is no longer allowed to go out with friends during the evenings and weekends. Her parents have told her she must concentrate on her education and have hired a private tutor, who comes to their home for an hour every weekday and four hours on Saturday and Sunday. Savita is not allowed to use the Internet; and her mother monitors what she does at home. Savita dreamed of a job as a doctor but is now coming to terms with the role of a housewife instead.

Scenario 11: *Surinderpal*

Surinderpal was feeling very stressed about a business decision. He went to his local gurdwara to find peace and pray. A friend sat next to him in the langar hall and, as they ate together, asked what the problem was. Surinderpal explained his problem; before he knew what was happening his friend had rung a *baba* (holy man) in India and told Surinderpal that he must listen and faithfully follow the advice given. Surinderpal was a bit sceptical but he was moved by the confidence and reverence with which his friend spoke about this *baba*.

Surinderpal followed the advice and his business did well over the next few months. One evening, he had a call from his friend, who said that he had a warning from Baba Ji in India. Baba Ji had seen terrible misfortunes in Surinderpal's future, which could only be prevented if he were to follow the new instructions to attend a special prayer group regularly and make recurring charitable donations to Baba Ji's *seva* (service) project.

Surinderpal has become increasingly involved with this group; they have become like his new family and he relies heavily on Baba Ji's instructions. He has lost contact with his friends and, due to increasing demands for charitable donations, there are tensions in his marriage.

Baba Ji has now instructed him to fulfil his spiritual destiny by selling his business and house and moving with his family to the *baba*'s *dera* (base) in Punjab to live as a full-time volunteer. Surinderpal's wife has said she will divorce him and keep the children in the UK if he tries to follow through. As sole owner of both the house and the business, he has told his wife that he will take all the money and move to India: Baba Ji has told him that this is a test of his faith and that only the most faithful receive salvation.

Abuse of volunteers

Volunteers are often very generous with what they give to their faith institution. Many see their service in their place of worship as part of their service to God, so they give sacrificially of their time, money and talents. But there are times when they are asked to give too much. One of the principles that defines a healthy organization is that they pay attention to the balance of exchange. There is a sense of equity between how much people give to their place of worship and how much they receive from it. In the case of volunteers, this balance will never involve money, but it will involve respect, maintaining appropriate boundaries, and space for personal spiritual devotion, work, other interests and family life, as well as not being asked to give more than they are able to.

There are questions of leadership style and how authority is used that lie behind these scenarios. They are deliberately much shorter than those in the previous section; they are written to provoke discussion as to what makes for a healthy culture in a faith community in relation to how volunteers are treated. Therefore, the scenarios that follow are not necessarily examples of spiritual abuse. They might simply be classified as poor practice in volunteer management or exploiting the goodwill of volunteers. As you read through the scenarios, discuss these questions:

- What is the experience of the person in the scenario?
- What is the perspective of the wider faith community, including the leadership?
- Does this scenario contain an element of spiritual abuse?

Nathan

Nathan has been a member of his *shul* (synagogue) since childhood. The congregation is very small. Their constitution states that no one can be the chair for more than three terms of office (nine years in total). Nathan has already been the chair for three terms, but no one wants to replace him. He does not want the role any more; he feels, however, that he has no option but to stand for a fourth term. Nathan also acts as the caretaker for the *shul*, as well as the fundraiser. He is about to retire and had been hoping to step back from these roles. He feels, though, that he has no choice but to continue in them.

Salma

Salma has been teaching at a local madrasa for the past 12 years. She began when her own children started at the madrasa because teachers did not have to pay for their own children to attend. She has continued teaching the same age group for all that time, even though her own children finished some time before. Although the madrasa charges a fee to parents, Salma is not paid. When she asked about this, the imam who oversees the madrasa explained that all the money goes on buying textbooks and paying for the mosque overheads. Salma knows that this is not true, as her husband, a member of the mosque committee, has told her that the madrasa contributes nothing to the mosque's running costs. Salma has noticed that the imam has a brand new car but feels guilty for wondering if the income from the madrasa has paid for it. Salma enjoys the teaching, and feels it is part of her service to Allah. But her family could also do with some extra income.

Narinder

Narinder has been attending her local gurdwara since she was a child. She is now in her 40s; her children have left home and she has started to go to the gurdwara during the week, as well as at weekends. A member of the management committee has asked Narinder to take charge of producing langar (free food from the community kitchen) for at least one day a week, if not more. Narinder is happy cooking for her own family but is not sure if she can oversee food production for an average of 70 people. Narinder has been told that the committee is relying on her and that her willingness to take on this role will be regarded as evidence of her devotion to Waheguru (Almighty God). Her husband has told her she must take on the role or he will be publicly shamed among his friends. Narinder is not sure what to do.

Dorothy

Dorothy has been attending her local Methodist Church for the past four years. She started coming because a friend invited her. She found the people she met there to be very friendly and welcoming. For the past two years, Dorothy has been helping at the Sunday School as an assistant. The church is very small; at most, there are six children attending a service. The children's ages range from 3 to 14. Because of a lack of volunteers, they are all in one group. The main leader has just stopped running the group because of ill health. Dorothy does not feel equipped to become the Sunday School teacher; a few of her friends, however, have told her that they think God is calling her to the role. 'God equips those he calls, dear, and he's definitely calling you', one of the stewards said to her last week. Dorothy does not know what to do.

Abuse of staff

Sometimes those who are employed by faith organizations are abused and this abuse may have a spiritual element. Those who run faith organizations are often not trained or experienced in HR matters; it may be that some simple training could go a long way to ensuring that abusive employment practices are prevented. To give a personal example, all the churches I have worked for have expected me to pay for and provide my own computer equipment in order to do my job. I would not class this as a type of spiritual abuse; but it does illustrate attitudes that are deemed acceptable in a religious context that would be unacceptable elsewhere. There is always a tension between the reality of 'what is' in a faith community and the ideal of 'what should be' in an employment context. We are unlikely to fully realize what should be, but that should not stop us trying to get closer to it. A key point in relation to the treatment of staff in faith organizations is the importance of training those in senior leadership roles in human resources and people management, as well as encouraging reflexivity and accountability. Think back to some of the Church of England case studies in Chapter 5. Poor employment practice features in several of them.

The following scenarios are all based on real-life situations, although the details and names have been changed. They are chosen to illustrate the difficulty of deciding what constitutes spiritual abuse and what is simply poor employment practice. As you read through, ask yourself these questions:

- How is the scenario experienced by the person described?
- What is the perspective of the leadership and of the faith community as a whole?

- Is there an element of spiritual abuse in this scenario?
- What should happen next?

Yusuf

Yusuf was educated in a private Islamic school. Then, at 16, he went to a *darul uloom* ('house of knowledge', an Islamic seminary), where he devoted himself to the study of the Qur'an and Arabic. He graduated eight years later, aged 24, and was offered a post as a junior imam in a mosque in his home town.

The post is unpaid but does come with housing. Yusuf is also expected to coordinate and teach at the mosque's madrasa, which runs for two hours a day. Yusuf is paid at the same rate as all the teachers: £4 per hour. He works as a care assistant, on a zero-hours contract, to supplement his income. He finds this work both rewarding and frustrating, as this was not what he spent so much of his life training to do.

Chris

Chris works part time for an evangelical Anglican church. The church is quite large, with a staff team of 12 people and an average Sunday attendance of 180 people across three services. Chris originally agreed to work for six hours a week but has never signed a contract of employment; nor has he had any formal agreement about his hours of work. Chris's main work responsibilities are in supporting the youth and children's work of the church. Chris also volunteers as a Sunday School teacher, for which no payment is made. The actual hours Chris works vary from none, during some weeks of the summer holidays, to 15, during particularly busy weeks. Chris is unhappy with the situation but is not sure what to do about it.

Sahan

Sahan is a Sri Lankan Buddhist monk. He has always wanted to visit England and was invited by a small, ex-pat community to visit them as their monk for a few months. They could not afford to pay him but were prepared to cover the costs of his flight and provide him with accommodation for three months. Sahan entered the country on a tourist visa; at the end of the three months, the community expect him to return to Sri Lanka. Sahan is two months into his stay in England and really wants it to be extended. He feels the community owe him the chance to become a permanent resident; however, they tell him they cannot afford it and expect him to leave in a month's time.

Jenny

Jenny is a Baptist minister. She has been in post for six months. When she came to 'preach with a view', she found the congregation to be very welcoming and friendly. But things have started to change recently. Two of the elders have talked openly in front of her about their disapproval of women preachers. The treasurer has complained, in a members' meeting, that Jenny's expenses are 'excessive'. Several of the elders' wives have told Jenny that she should not wear trousers when leading a service, as such behaviour is 'unbecoming of a woman'. Jenny is single and feels she cannot start looking for a new job already. This is her first post, so she knows she needs to stay longer before moving on. But she also thinks she has made a big mistake in accepting this job.

9

Sample Sermons for Safeguarding Sunday

The third Sunday of November has been established as Safeguarding Sunday. In this chapter, I offer three sermons, with the lectionary readings, for preachers to use. Obviously, this chapter is aimed at Christian preachers. If that is not you, how could you share a message about safeguarding in your own context?

Year A sermon for Safeguarding Sunday

Readings: Zephaniah 1.7, 12–18; Psalm 90.1–12; Matthew 25.14–30; 1 Thessalonians 5.1–11

Safeguarding is one of those endless tasks that requires continuous vigilance. It is a task that is never complete. The other day, I was talking with someone about a complicated pastoral matter. It's not appropriate to give even vague details. Leicester is a small city and even an outline might give too much away. At the time, I focused on listening and supporting the person to make what seemed to be the best choice for their own situation. It was only as things unfolded, and I thought further, that I realized I needed to make a safeguarding referral. I duly did so and had a helpful conversation with one of the team. We agreed on what I should do, and that was that.

I have never had a job where I have not had to make safeguarding referrals at one time or another. Even when I first started out as a pastoral assistant, there were some things that came up in the youth groups I helped to run. After every session, the leaders met and one of the questions we always asked was, 'Does anyone have a safeguarding referral?' The point was to make it normal and natural: just a part of our culture of debriefing after a session. This meant that when something did come up, we were ready to deal with it because we were expecting, at some point, that we would have to. The same has been true throughout my ministry of supporting and working with the congregations of different churches. Even in my current role, where I am in many different churches, there are still opportunities to talk about safeguarding, to support congregations to do the right thing, and to make sure the people of God care for the least and the most vulnerable within their communities. For we are all accountable to God for how we live.

Our reading from Zephaniah is a warning about divine judgement. As the commentator O. Palmer Robertson puts it: 'Particularly the uninvolved, the indifferent, and the sceptical are selected for condemnation' (Robertson, 1990, p. 280). The work these people do will be of no lasting value; they will suffer punishment when the day of the Lord comes. People may think that meeting God will be cheerful but, in Zephaniah's vision, there is a terrifying theophany in which the overflowing wrath of God is unleashed. Robertson quotes a hymn by Thomas of Celano:

> That day of wrath, that dreadful day
> When heav'n and earth shall pass away!
> What pow'r shall be the sinner's stay?
> How shall he meet that dreadful day?
>
> When, shrivelling like a parched scroll,
> The flaming heav'ns together roll;
> When louder yet, and yet more dread,
> Swells the high trump that wakes the dead;
>
> O on that day, that wrathful day
> When man to judgement wakes from clay,
> Be thou the trembling sinner's stay,
> Though heav'n and earth shall pass away.
> (Robertson, 1990, p. 283)

Judgement cannot be avoided. All will be held accountable for their actions.

After reading the past case reviews of several Anglican instances of serious and horrific child abuse, as well as other forms of abusive behaviour, it strikes me that the perpetrators believed themselves to be beyond judgement. They thought they were free from the judgement of people; and there is no sense that they held themselves accountable before God.

While we might find Zephaniah's words challenging and may struggle with his concept of the day of God's wrath and judgement, there is certainly space for sober reflection on our actions. We need to think about the consequences of choosing to act and, maybe more seriously, not doing so because of indifference, excessive busyness or just not seeing something as sufficiently important to warrant our attention. Many of the reviews into safeguarding failures note that, at an early stage, there were signs that something was not quite right; yet no one did anything about it.

Psalm 90 is a prayer in the face of divine judgement. John Eaton suggests that the people are suffering because of God's wrath at some unspecified sin. The psalmist reflects on the transitory nature of human life, especially in the face of divine eternity. People are like fragile Palestinian plants that flourish in the morning but by the evening are withered and dry. The people are suffering and distressed; they come to God, who they believe is punishing them for their misdemeanours, and appeal to him to meet them with justice and mercy (Eaton, 2005, p. 323). We should not read this psalm as teaching us that abuse is a punishment for sin. Rather, it is those who perpetrate abuse that will be subject to divine judgement. The consistent theme of all our readings is that actions have consequences. We will be held accountable before God for how we have chosen to live and for the results of those choices.

Our Gospel reading, Matthew 25.14–30, centres on this theme. Verses 14–15 introduce the underlying idea: the absence of the master (who represents Jesus, the Son of Man) and the interim responsibility of the servants (disciples). The point is that we are held to account for our actions; it is not enough to say that we are followers of Jesus. We must demonstrate we are by how we live.

It's easy to get distracted by the money in this passage. One talent was 6,000 denarii (or 20 years' wages, so say £500,000). But the main question concerns what we do with what God gives us. It is not only about money but also about the stewardship of gifts and abilities. Thus, the doubling of the money in verses 16 to 18 speaks, within the world of the parable, of actual, active discipleship. The contrast between the first two servants and the third is that the third servant makes no gain, not even from a token investment in a bank: he merely conserves. He displays only lip service discipleship.

There follows the settling of accounts, which represents eschatological judgement. The 'joy of your master' is a sign of eschatological blessing. Faithfulness in small things – which includes in our context attending safeguarding training, keeping good records, developing a healthy and open culture – is rewarded at the end of time.

The lazy servant attempts to justify himself in verses 24 to 25. But there are no excuses. This servant is wicked because of his bad stewardship. His culpability is greater because he knew his master expected profit. He therefore faces judgement. Even the little he has is taken from him, as he is cast out of God's presence.

What's the point of the parable? To scare us into action.

Fear is a good motivator: we could see this at work during the Covid-19 virus outbreak. Fear of getting ill motivated people to stockpile food, wash their hands more, and so on. Politicians use fear: it was a tactic in the 2019 and 2024 general elections.

Jesus does not just use fear to motivate us. His primary means is self-sacrificial love. But he does want us to be aware of the consequences of not living out our discipleship to the full. When Jesus uses fear, it is fear in the sense of a right and true recognition of the holiness of God, our dependence upon him for salvation and our duty to obey.

Perhaps a helpful way of thinking about this is to look at how the Apostle Paul encourages the Christians in Thessalonica.

A helpful passage to hold in tension with the parable of Jesus is 1 Thessalonians 5.1–11. It says to me that if we wilfully disobey God, we will be cast out of his presence at the end of time, which is a logical consequence. If you choose to ignore God, why do you expect God to be interested in you?

But what Paul is saying is that if we try to serve God, then we will be ready for Jesus when he returns. We must diligently do the work of disciples whatever our circumstances, whatever the challenges we are facing. This brings us to the crucial question: the third servant does nothing because he does not trust the master: he is just scared of him. The other two servants took risks because they trusted.

Over the past few years, I have been working with colleagues from a range of religious backgrounds to develop ways of improving safeguarding policy and practice in places of worship. This has included conversations about spiritual abuse. One of the people I talked to said:

> The impact of abuse can always be damaging. The impact of abuse in a spiritual setting has the capacity to go even deeper than any other type of abuse ... If we have ascribed spiritual leadership to an individual, that seems to go hand in hand with a fairly deep level of trust. So, if the person in that spiritual place then takes advantage of that trust and is abusive ... it seems to also hit something even deeper around our level of trust. And that becomes a hugely destabilizing factor in somebody's sense of certainty and solidity about life.

All forms of abuse are destructive. Spiritual abuse especially so. This is because spiritual abuse destroys the ability of individuals and groups to trust. And where there is no trust, there is no certainty and life cannot flourish. As Brené Brown observes:

> Betrayal is so painful because, at its core, it is a violation of trust. It happens in relationships in which trust is expected and assumed, so when it is violated, we're often shocked, and we can struggle to believe what's happening. It can feel as if the ground beneath us has given way. (Brown, 2021, p. 194)

I think this describes the experiences of those who have been abused. Our Bible readings today remind us that we are all accountable before God for how we live, what we support, what we challenge, what we ignore, and what we file as 'too difficult' and try to forget about.

Today is Safeguarding Sunday. But safeguarding is not a once-a-year thing: it is an everyday, all-the-time thing. As we reflect on our readings and on the charge that God has given us, let us resolve to be people who live in the light, always working to keep others safe as part of our service to our Lord and Master; to use what he has given us for his glory and to build his kingdom.

A moment of quiet and then I will pray.

Year B sermon for Safeguarding Sunday

Readings: Daniel 12.1–3; Psalm 16; Hebrews 10.11–25; Mark 13.1–8

I can vividly remember a conversation I had with a primary school head teacher. I was the chair of governors, as well as the safeguarding lead for the governing body. Although it was only a small school, the nature of the area meant there were a lot of safeguarding referrals, several every week. As such, it was very unusual for the head teacher and me to have any detailed conversations about specific cases. There simply wasn't the time. Moreover, it would not have been appropriate for me to know any details. In fact, most of the time, I knew nothing at all about the cases. My role, after all, was primarily to ensure the system was functioning properly; that teachers and ancillary staff knew their roles and were fulfilling them.

The reason we were having the conversation was because a child had made a safeguarding disclosure to a teaching assistant. But this teaching assistant had not taken the disclosure seriously; they had brushed it off as an example of the pupil's bad behaviour rather than recognizing the incident for what it was, namely an incident of physical abuse. The reason the head teacher and I were talking was not to blame this individual; rather, it was to work out how the school could develop a healthier culture in which tackling safeguarding issues was normalized and made a part of everyday life. The teaching assistant had attended the annual safeguarding refresher course earlier in the academic year; but it was not enough for safeguarding to be embedded in her approach to her job. Much more work was needed to develop a healthy culture in that school.

The same is true of many other organizations. We all know safeguarding is important. We ensure that the relevant people have appropriate DBS checks. We attend training. We put information about safeguarding in a prominent place on our websites. We even appoint an independent person to oversee safeguarding. But is safeguarding part of our culture, a normalized aspect of the way we do things around here?

The reality is that safeguarding incidents do not come neatly packaged and labelled. Someone says something; we have milliseconds to react. Unless safeguarding is embedded and instinctive, that reaction may not be the most helpful or useful. We may, like the teaching assistant mentioned earlier, react badly and miss the opportunity. That is, of course, not the end of the world. If we recognize our mistake, there are opportunities to mitigate and make amends. But it would be better if we did not make the mistake in the first place and reacted appropriately to any disclosures of abuse.

What do our readings say about safeguarding? How can they help us to develop a healthy church culture?

The short portion from Daniel 12 is one of the visions the seer has: in this case, a vision of divine judgement on the guilty and vindication for the righteous. Daniel is a complicated book to understand in detail, but the main message is clear. Although it may not look like it, God is in control. Michael is an angel, the spiritual protector of God's people. Even though they suffer, Michael will protect and care for them; he will ultimately bring them to eternity with God. As Tremper Longman puts it: 'though prospering in the present, the wicked will get their due, and, though suffering in the present, the godly will get their reward. God will see to it' (Longman, 1999, p. 292).

When thinking about safeguarding, perhaps the key verse is

'There shall be a time of anguish, such as has never occurred since nations first came into existence' (v. 1). I personally have not experienced abuse; but when I listen to those who have, they talk of devastation, of anguish that is unending and apparently unstoppable. Saying 'God is in control' can seem like trite nonsense, especially to those who have been abused by priests or other religious authority figures. Some have been so harmed by the Church that they walk away from faith entirely. Somehow, amid the suffering and pain, we have to find ways of listening, of caring, of supporting and, when the time is right, of speaking of God's justice and his love. For as verse 3 promises, a time of redemption and healing will come. We must cling fast to that promise when evil threatens to overwhelm us.

Psalm 16 is a 'prayer for the Lord's protection ... supported by eloquent statements of loyalty and close fellowship with God' (Eaton, 2005, p. 97). The psalmist has experienced trouble, strife and difficulty. He has seen the prosperity of the wicked. But nevertheless, he has remained faithful to the God who preserves and protects his life. Some people can hold on to God in even the most terrible of situations. Over the past few years, I have had lots of conversations with people about spiritual abuse. A recurrent theme from some is that abuse is perpetrated by people who pervert and distort God's teachings, actions and character. Psalm 16 helps us to keep a right vision of God as protector, provider and carer for all of us. Although those who abuse may distort and destroy understandings of God, Scripture can be the means of restoring our vision and relationship with the God who loves us, who has saved us and who will make all things perfect.

Hebrews 10 reminds us of the once-for-all perfect sacrifice of Christ on the cross, of how he has enabled us to approach the throne of grace with the humble confidence that God hears us and cares for us. We do not need anyone to mediate our access to God; we can go directly to him.

Abuse can be characterized by coercive control, by individuals putting themselves up as the sole mediator between God and me. Lisa Oakley and Justin Humphreys define spiritual abuse in this way:

Spiritual abuse is a form of emotional and psychological abuse. It is characterized by a systematic pattern of coercive and controlling behaviour in a religious context. Spiritual abuse can have a deeply damaging impact on those who experience it.

This abuse may include: manipulation and exploitation, enforced accountability, censorship of decision making, requirements for secrecy and silence, coercion to conform, control through the use of sacred texts or teaching, requirement of obedience to the abuser, the suggestion that the abuser has a 'divine' position, isolation as a means of punishment, and superiority and elitism. (Oakley and Humphreys, 2019, p. 31)

Hebrews 10 reminds us that all that is necessary for our salvation has already been completed by Christ. The epistle makes this point numerous times. It argues that repeated sacrifices are not needed any more, for everything is fulfilled in Christ. Believers can approach the throne of grace with a clear conscience (Johnson, 2006, p. 254). Robust confidence in the efficacy of Christ's finished work is a potential defence against exploitation and forms of spiritual abuse.

Mark 13 is best understood as Jesus' farewell to his followers. He combines prophecy about the future with an exhortation to the Disciples on how to live when their Master is no longer with them. The main function of this text is to promote faith and obedience in a time of distress and upheaval (Lane, 1974, pp. 444–6). Jesus reminds us of the reality of false teachers, those who claim to be godly but whose actions reveal that, in fact, they are not. To pick up Jesus' words, these people are wolves in sheep's clothing who disguise themselves as righteous but whose behaviour, attitude and actions all display their affinity to the evil in this world. The text also reminds us of the temporary nature of life: things we may believe to be permanent will not actually last, be they buildings or be they terrible situations; all will eventually be swept away when creation is renewed and made perfect.

But what do we do while we wait? What is the place of safeguarding within the Church? It is of foundational and fundamental importance. People – even those who never join us for worship – expect Christians to be people of integrity and grace; people who promote the care of orphans, widows and the destitute. We can take this to indicate an expectation that the Church will care for all who are vulnerable. The sad truth is, of course, that this is not the case. I well remember a conversation with an official in the Crown Prosecution Service who explained that, although she was culturally Christian, she would never let her children attend church because she regarded it as 'a holiday camp for paedophiles'. Sadly, every few months, another case hits the headlines and her point is reinforced. Whether it is a residentiary canon at Blackburn Cathedral (Maqbool and Swann, 2024) or a well-known charismatic youth leader (Maqbool, 2024), the drip, drip of shameful scandal continues.

We may not be able to deal with those big problems. But we can take responsibility for what happens in our own contexts. Although much has been done to embed safeguarding in church culture, there remains plenty more to do. While recognizing that, ultimately, we are accountable to the Lord for our actions done in his name, let us resolve to continue the work of safeguarding children and adults at risk. Let us ensure that all may flourish and attain the fullness of life that Christ promises for all who follow him.

A moment of quiet and then I will pray.

Year C sermon for Safeguarding Sunday

Readings: Malachi 4.1–2a; Psalm 98; 2 Thessalonians 3.6–13; Luke 21.5–19

Looking at reports and past case reviews, issues of safeguarding appear very black and white. There is a correct answer or responsible action, but it was not taken. Why is that? Perhaps it is more accurate to say that while abuse is categorically always wrong, questions around safeguarding become a little bit more complicated.

Professor Lisa Oakley has developed a great tool for helping us to unpack this issue. It's a continuum of behaviours, from healthy, to unhelpful, to unhealthy, to abusive. The Church of England guidance on safeguarding explains further, using the example of financial giving (see Table 1 on p. 18).

The continuum applies to a wide variety of issues, where subjectivity creeps in. To give another example, when is seeking guidance from your priest healthy and when has it tipped over into unhelpful behaviour? When is a mentoring relationship good and healthy and when does it become controlling and abusive?

It would be wonderful if we all lived in a very black-and-white world, where everything was straightforward and clear; one where we knew what was right and what was wrong. Our short reading from Malachi points to such a world. Malachi sees the coming judgement of God and he divides people into two groups. Those who do evil, those who ignore the Lord and his teaching will be burnt up as in an oven. But those who revere God's name will have the sun of righteousness rise upon them, with healing in his wings (see Mal. 4.2). One commentator proposes: 'Surely the rays of the sun must be behind the expression "the Lord make his face to shine upon you" in the priestly blessing' of Numbers 6.24–6 (Smith, 1984, p. 339). Christians inevitably hear this as talking about the birth, life, death and Resurrection of Jesus Christ. The original Jewish audience heard it differently; but the same point underlies their understanding as well. God will act to bring about righteousness and restoration. In the context of discussions of safeguarding, that means perpetrators of abuse will face judgement not just now but in the life to come as well.

Psalm 98 makes the same point. The Lord is worthy of praise because of all that he has done. God has acted decisively, bringing healing and wholeness, as well as judgement and deliverance. The people who have received divine mercy praise him for his kindness to them. Even the natural world praises God for his manifest justice and righteousness. 'The Lord is revealed in his temple, victorious and supreme, faithful and bearing salvation, at the outset of a reign of right, the inauguration of the kingdom of all that is good' (Eaton, 2005, p. 345).

But what does our reading from Paul's second letter to the Thessalonians say about safeguarding? On a cursory reading, probably not a lot. The challenge in understanding Paul's letters is in working out what the issues are that he is responding to. Paul is not writing to the church in Thessalonica for the fun of it: he is writing to answer questions and to respond to issues he has become aware of. The process of working out exactly what has happened is called mirror reading. It is always a guess; and scholars debate what the right guess is. Gradually, over time a consensus forms as scholars with different perspectives agree on what they think the problem is. In this case, the best guess is this: some of those who have recently become Christians are so caught up in waiting for the Lord's return that they have given up on everything, including work. What has happened is that there are some super-spiritual people who spend all their time praying for the Lord's return while expecting other people to do all the hard work of earning money and providing for their needs. Or perhaps people are just being lazy and using their alleged religious fervour as an excuse to do nothing. The Bible scholar F. F. Bruce suggests that maybe those who are not working are stirring up trouble and interfering in other people's business (Bruce, 1982, pp. 208–9).

Paul says that this is unacceptable and if people want to eat, they need to work with their own hands. Of course, that does not mean those who are not able to work should be punished. Elsewhere, Paul talks about the necessary work of charity for those who cannot provide for themselves. His point here is that we all have a responsibility to do what we are called to do and that includes working, when possible, to provide for ourselves and those who depend upon us. And it is here that we can see a principle at work behind Paul's answer that applies to safeguarding.

There is a necessary work to be done in protecting children and all those who are vulnerable or at risk of abuse. We must not shirk that responsibility, however onerous it might be, however much we would rather be doing other things. Safeguarding is not a nice extra to have, a little bit of icing on the cake of ministry. Rather, it is a fundamental ingredient for wholesome, healthy Christian culture. A Church that is not interested in the weak and the vulnerable is a Church that has departed from the teaching of Jesus Christ. Safeguarding is a must-do, not a nice-to-do, thing. It is difficult, complicated, messy and challenging. But that is no reason not to do it.

It is also not immediately obvious what the Gospel reading from Luke has to say about safeguarding. Jesus is teaching in the temple. In fact, he has just been watching people put money in the temple treasury and commended a poor widow for giving all she had. He suggests that those who have given merely from their surplus have not understood what it is to give sacrificially in God's service.

While they were talking about sacrificial giving, Jesus' Disciples delighted in the fixtures and furnishings of the temple. Jesus tells them it will not last. He warns them of trouble ahead: that there will be wars, calamities, difficulties, false messiahs; all sorts of problems. Those who follow Jesus with all they have will be subject to trials, persecution and hatred. The passage is a call to endure, a command to faithfulness amid opposition and struggle. As the commentator Joel Green explains, 'Thematically, Jesus' discourse underscores the faithful hand of God in the series of events to unfold and the call for concomitant human faithfulness' (Green, 1997, p. 732).

And it is here that we can discern a principle that applies to safeguarding, namely the cost of speaking truth to power. Making a safeguarding disclosure, exposing a perpetrator's actions is a difficult and painful thing in and of itself. What makes it exponentially harder is when that disclosure is not believed; when people unite not to defend and support the victims but, rather, to further persecute, punish and harm them.

I have never had to disclose personal experience of abuse, but talking with those who have, one theme that emerges is that of not being heard, of not being believed. People are put on trial for doing the right thing, for speaking out about the injustice they have experienced, for explicitly naming sexual abuse as abuse. There are so many well-publicized cases of this great sin within the Anglican Church. To name a few: Bishop Peter Ball used his establishment connections to cast doubt on the disclosures of those he had abused. Those who reported the inappropriate behaviour of the Soul Survivor leader Mike Pilavachi were similarly met with a wall of silence or had their disclosures of abuse dismissed with 'That's just Mike'. A similar phrase, 'It's just Jonathan', was used in reference to Jonathan Fletcher's inappropriate behaviour and actions. I could go on. There are many other cases that do not receive the publicity but whose damage is as great. The point is plain: there is a cost to speaking truth; but if we do not have to bear that cost ourselves, we must be alert to ensure that we do not make it worse. We must act to support our fellow Christians and, indeed, anybody who has experienced abuse, as they seek justice.

All of us are accountable for our own choices and actions. When we witness something that is clearly wrong, we have a duty to speak out, even if there will be a price to be paid. Where things are more complicated, we have a duty to keep questioning, to bring the light of God's truth into the darker corners of the Church, for the well-being of all. Let us ask for the Spirit's help as we seek to live God's way.

A moment of quiet and then I will pray.

Conclusion: The Way Forward

Spiritual abuse is real. Even if you don't accept this expression, the actions and their impact are clear. My purpose in writing this book has been to reflect theologically and practically on the risks and reality of spiritual abuse. I have done so in four ways:

1 by developing the understanding of spiritual abuse and setting out my methodological and ethical approach to my research;
2 by sharing voices from the first and second phases of my research. I developed my theory that agency and education provide a suitable response to the risks and realities of spiritual abuse;
3 by discussing lessons from six Church of England case studies of spiritual abuse. I also reflected theologically from a Christian perspective on how best to respond;
4 by suggesting next steps. I discussed how to work with the authorities, wrote sample sermons, and shared ideas for an awareness-raising workshop and case studies for further reflection.

The key point is to do something. Spiritual abuse is sadly a reality in faith-based organizations. It is not enough to recognize the reality: we must act.

Bibliography

Allport, Gordon, 1954, *The Nature of Prejudice*, Cambridge, MA: Addison-Wesley.
Ally, Safiyyah, 2022, 'Tackling Spiritual Abuse', *Let the Quran Speak*, 24 July 2022, https://www.quranspeaks.com/post/spiritual-abuse, accessed 20.2.2025.
Ammerman, Nancy T., 'Spiritual but not Religious? Beyond binary choices in the study of religion', *Journal for the Scientific Study of Religion*, 52 2 (2013), pp. 258–78.
Arbuckle, Gerald A., 2019, *Abuse and Cover-Up: Refounding the Catholic Church in Trauma*, Maryknoll, NY: Orbis Books.
Astley, Jeff, 2002, *Ordinary Theology: Looking, Listening and Learning in Theology*, Farnham: Ashgate.
Astley, Jeff and Leslie J. Francis (eds), 2013, *Exploring Ordinary Theology: Everyday Christian Believing and the Church*, Farnham: Ashgate.
Baker, W. R., *Personal Speech: Ethics in the Epistle of James*, Tübingen: Mohr, 1995.
Ballard, Paul, and John Pritchard, 2006, *Practical Theology in Action: Christian Thinking in the Service of Church and Society*, 2nd edn, London: SPCK.
Barclay, J. M. G., 1988, *Obeying the Truth: A Study of Paul's Ethics in Galatians*, Edinburgh: T&T Clark.
Barnett, Paul, 1997, *The Second Epistle to the Corinthians*, The New International Commentary on the New Testament, Grand Rapids, MI: Eerdmans.
Barron, Lynsey M., and William P. Eiselstein, 2021, 'Report of Independent Investigation into Sexual Misconduct of Ravi Zacharias', *Courthouse News Service*, 9 February 2021, https://www.courthousenews.com/wp-content/uploads/2021/02/zacharias-report.pdf, accessed 20.02.2025.
Bayfield, Tony (ed.), 2017, *Deep Calls to Deep: Transforming Conversations between Jews and Christians*, London: SCM Press.
Beaumont, Catherine, 2020, *Supporting Adult Survivors of Child Sexual Abuse: A Mimetic Theory Approach for the Local Church*, London: Jessica Kingsley Publishing.

Berkovits, Shira M., 'Institutional Abuse in the Jewish Community', *Tradition: A Journal of Orthodox Jewish Thought*, 50 2 (2017), pp. 11–49.
Betz, H. D., 1979, *A Commentary on Paul's Letter to the Churches in Galatia*, Philadelphia, PA: Fortress Press.
Bibb, Bryan D., 'Nadab and Abihu Attempt to Fill a Gap: Law and narrative in Leviticus 10.1–7', *Journal for the Study of the Old Testament*, 96 (2001), pp. 83–99.
Bierman, Alex, 'The Effects of Childhood Maltreatment on Adult Religiosity and Spirituality: Rejecting God the Father because of abusive fathers?', *Journal for the Scientific Study of Religion*, 44 3 (2005), pp. 349–59.
Blau, Yosef, 'Sexual Abuse in the Orthodox Jewish Community', *Tradition: A Journal of Orthodox Jewish Thought*, 50 2 (2017), pp. 50–9.
Blue, Ken, 1993, *Healing Spiritual Abuse: How to Break Free from Bad Church Experiences*, Downers Grove, IL: IVP Books.
Brown, Brené, 2021, *Atlas of the Heart: Mapping Meaningful Connection and the Language of Human Experience*, London: Vermillion.
Bruce, F. F., 1982, *1 and 2 Thessalonians*, Word Biblical Commentary 45, Nashville, TN: Thomas Nelson.
Cameron, Helen D., 2018, *Living in the Gaze of God*, London: SCM Press.
Cares, Alison C., and Gretchen R. Cusick, 'Risks and Opportunities of Faith and Culture: The case of abused Jewish women', *Journal of Family Violence*, 27 (2012), pp. 427–35.
Casey, P. M., 'Culture and Historicity: The cleansing of the temple', *The Catholic Biblical Quarterly*, 59 (1997), pp. 306–32.
Cashwell, Craig S., and Paula J. Swindle, 'When Religion Hurts: Supervising cases of religious abuse', *The Clinical Supervisor*, 37 (2018), pp. 182–203.
Charmaz, Kathy, 2006, *Constructing Grounded Theory: A Practical Guide Through Qualitative Analysis*, London: Sage Publications.
Charmaz, Kathy, 2021, 'The Genesis, Grounds, and Growth of Constructivist Grounded Theory', in Janice M. Morse, Barbara J. Bowers, Kathy Charmaz, Adele E. Clarke, Juliet Cobin and Carline Jane Porr, with Phyllis Noerager Stern (eds), *Developing Grounded Theory: The Second Generation Revisited*, 2nd edn, London: Routledge, pp. 153–87.
Chowdhury, Rahmanara, Belinda Winder, Nicholas Blagden and Farooq Mulla, 2021, '"I Thought in Order to Get to God I Had to Win Their Approval": A qualitative analysis of the experiences of Muslim victims abused by religious authority figures', *Journal of Sexual Aggression*, 28 (2022), pp. 196–217.
Church of England, 2017, 'Tribunal for the Diocese of Oxford, The Venerable Judith French Complainant and The Reverend Timothy Davis Respondent', uploaded 28 December 2018, https://www.churchofeng

BIBLIOGRAPHY

land.org/sites/default/files/2018-01/td-judgement-final-20181228.pdf, accessed 20.02.2025.

Church of England, 2020, 'Archbishop of Canterbury Announces 2020 Lambeth Awards Recipients', *The Archbishop of Canterbury*, 30 June 2020, https://www.archbishopofcanterbury.org/news/news-and-statements/archbishop-canterbury-announces-2020-lambeth-awards-recipients, accessed 20.02.2025.

Church of England, 2021, *Safeguarding e-manual*, https://www.churchofengland.org/safeguarding/safeguarding-e-manual/safeguarding-children-young-people-and-vulnerable-adults/42#_ftn1, accessed 20.02.2025.

Church of England, 2023, 'Concerns Substantiated in Mike Pilavachi Investigation', 6 September 2023, https://www.churchofengland.org/media/press-releases/concerns-substantiated-mike-pilavachi-investigation, accessed 20.02.2025.

Cochrane, Hilary, and Trudi Newton, 2018, *Supervision and Coaching: Growth and Learning in Professional Practice*, London: Routledge.

Cohen, Michael H., 'Healing at the Borderland of Medicine and Religion: Regulating potential abuse of authority by spiritual healers', *Journal of Law and Religion*, 18 2 (2002), pp. 373–426.

Coleridge, Mark, 'The Sex Abuse Crisis and the Culture of the Church', *The Furrow*, 61 9 (2010), pp. 463–71.

Collins, Stella, 2019, *Neuroscience for Learning and Development: How to Apply Neuroscience and Psychology for Improved Learning and Training*, London: Kogan Page.

Creamer, Elizabeth G., 2022, *Developing Grounded Theory with Mixed Methods*, London: Routledge.

Dasa, Bhaktavatsala, 1999, 'Best Intentions – Dynamics of Spiritual Abuse', *Iskcon Communications*, 2 December 1999, https://www.iskconcommunications.org/iskcon-journal/vol-7/best-intentions-—-dynamics-of-spiritual-abuse, accessed 20.02.2025.

Dehan, Nicole, and Zipi Levi, 'Spiritual Abuse: An additional dimension of abuse experienced by abused Haredi (Ultraorthodox) Jewish wives', *Violence Against Women*, 15 11 (2009), pp. 1294–310.

Deken, Alice, 'Does Prophecy Cause History? Jeremiah 36: a scroll ablaze', *Old Testament Essays*, 30 3 (2017), pp. 630–52.

Denis, Jeffrey, 'Contact Theory in a Small-Town Settler-Colonial Context: The reproduction of laissez-faire racism in Indigenous–White Canadian relations', *American Sociological Review*, 15 (2015), pp. 218–42.

Dorr, Donal, 'Sexual Abuse and Spiritual Abuse', *The Furrow*, 51 10 (2000), pp. 523–31.

Duckworth, Angela, 2016, *Grit: Why Passion and Perseverance Are the Secrets to Success*, London: Vermilion.

Dunn, J. D. G., 1993, *The Epistle to the Galatians*, London: A&C Black.

Eaton, John, 2005, *The Psalms: A Historical and Spiritual Commentary with an Introduction and New Translation*, London: Continuum.

Edmondson, Amy C., 2019, *The Fearless Organization*, Hoboken, NJ: Wiley.
Erooga, Marcus, 2018, *Protecting Children and Adults from Abuse after Savile: What Organisations and Institutions Need to Do*, London: Jessica Kingsley Publishing.
Evangelical Alliance, 2018, *Reviewing the Discourse of 'Spiritual Abuse': Logical Problems and Unintended Consequences*, London: Evangelical Alliance.
Everett, Jim, 2013, 'Intergroup Contact Theory: Past, present and future', *The Inquisitive Mind*, https://www.in-mind.org/article/intergroup-contact-theory-past-present-and-future, accessed 20.02.2025.
Fernández, Samuel, 'Victims Are Not Guilty! Spiritual abuse and ecclesiastical responsibility', *Religions*, 13 5 (2022), p. 427–37, https://www.mdpi.com/2077-1444/13/5/427, accessed 19.06.2025.
Fife, Janet, and Gilo (eds), 2019, *Letters to a Broken Church*, London: Ekklesia.
France, R. T., 1989, *Matthew: Evangelist and Teacher*, Carlisle: Paternoster.
France, R. T., 2007, *The Gospel of Matthew*, The New International Commentary on the New Testament, Grand Rapids, MI: Eerdmans.
Gale, Aaron M., 2005, *Redefining Ancient Borders: The Jewish Scribal Framework of Matthew's Gospel*, London: T&T Clark.
Gale, Aaron M., 2017, 'The Gospel According to Matthew', in Amy-Jill Levine and Marc Zvi Brettler (eds), *The Jewish Annotated New Testament*, 2nd edn, Oxford: Oxford University Press, pp. 9–66.
Gall, Terry Lynn, Viola Basque, Marizete Damasceno-Scott and Gerard Vardy, 'Spirituality and the Current Adjustment of Adult Survivors of Childhood Sexual Abuse', *Journal for the Scientific Study of Religion*, 46 (2007), pp. 101–17.
Gierman-Riblon, Catherine, and Sandra Salloway, 'Teaching Interprofessionalism to Nursing Students: A learning experience based on Allport's Intergroup Contact Theory', *Nursing Education Perspectives*, 34 (2013), pp. 59–62.
Glaser, Barney, and Anselm Straus, 1967, *The Discovery of Grounded Theory: Strategies for Qualitative Research*, New York: De Gruyter.
Graystone, Andrew, 2021, *Bleeding for Jesus: John Smyth and the Cult of the Iwerne Camps*, London: Darton, Longman and Todd.
Green, Joel, 1997, *The Gospel of Luke*, The New International Commentary on the New Testament, Grand Rapids, MI: Eerdmans.
Groenewald, Alphonso, '"But let justice roll down like waters, and righteousness like an ever-flowing stream" (Am 5:24): Social justice versus cult criticism in Amos (5:21–24) and Isaiah (1:10–20) – a trauma perspective', *HTS Theological Studies*, 75 3 (2019), pp. 1–10.
Hagner, Donald A., 1995, *Matthew 14–28*, Word Biblical Commentary 33B, Dallas, TX: Word Books.

Hess, Richard S., 'Leviticus 10.1: Strange fire and an odd name', *Bulletin for Biblical Research*, 12 2 (2002), pp. 187–98.
Heyd, Andrew, 'Honor in the Cult: Leviticus 10 in socio-rhetorical perspective', *Journal for the Study of the Old Testament*, 46 4 (2022), pp. 548–62.
Heyder, Regina, 'Narrating and Remembrance in the Face of Abuse in the Church', *Religions*, 13 4 (2022), pp. 348–60.
Hilton, Michael, and Gordian Marshall, 1988, *The Gospels and Rabbinic Judaism: A Study Guide*, London: SCM Press.
Hodge, David R., and Charlene C. McGrew, 'Spirituality, Religion and the Interrelationship: A nationally representative study', *Journal of Social Work Education*, 42 3 (2006), pp. 637–54.
Home Office, 2022a, *Controlling or Coercive Behaviour: Statutory Guidance – What the Police and Organisations Should Do to Keep Victims Safe*, April 2022, https://assets.publishing.service.gov.uk/media/6267c4 29e90e071698 2a3250/ContCoerBehavStatGuid_V3-_10-04-22_.pdf, accessed 20.02.2025.
Home Office, 2022b, 'Positions of Trust: Police, Crime, Sentencing and Courts Act 2022 factsheet', *GOV.UK*, https://www.gov.uk/government/publications/police-crime-sentencing-and-courts-bill-2021-factsheets/police-crime-sentencing-and-courts-bill-2021-positions-of-trust-fact sheet, accessed 20.02.2025.
Hopkinson, Elaine, and Patrick Hopkinson, 2023, 'Lessons learnt from the historic events in the parish of St Margaret's, Tylers Green', https://d3hgrlq6yacptf.cloudfront.net/61f2fd86foee5/content/pages/documents/learning-lessons-review-revd-michael-hall-tylers-green.pdf, accessed 18.06.2025.
Houston, Walter, 'Tragedy in the Courts of the Lord: A socio-literary reading of the death of Nadab and Abihu', *Journal for the Study of the Old Testament*, 90 (2000), pp. 31–9.
Huys, Marc, 'Turning the Tables: Jesus' temple cleansing and the story of Lycaon', *Ephemerides Theologicae Lovanienses*, 86 (2010), pp. 137–61.
Hyman, Corine, and Paul J. Handal, 'Definitions and Evaluation of Religion and Spirituality Items by Religious Professionals: A pilot study', *Journal of Religion and Health*, 45 2 (2006), pp. 264–82.
IICSA, 2019, *Anglican Church Case Studies: Chichester/Peter Ball Investigation Report*, London: Independent Inquiry into Child Sexual Abuse.
IICSA, 2021, *Child Protection in Religious Organisations and Settings: Investigation Report*, London: Independent Inquiry into Child Sexual Abuse.
Jeremias, Jörg, 1998, *Old Testament Library: The Book of Amos*, Louisville, KY: Westminster John Knox Press.
Johnson, David, and Jeff VanVonderen, 1991, *The Subtle Power of Spiritual Abuse*, Minneapolis, MN: Bethany House Publishers.

Johnson, G., K. Scholes and R. Whittington, 2008, *Exploring Corporate Strategy: Text and Cases*, 8th edn, Harlow: Pearson Education.

Johnson, Jessica, 2018, *Biblical Porn: Affect, Labor, and Pastor Mark Driscoll's Evangelical Empire*, Durham, NC: Duke University Press.

Johnson, Luke Timothy, 2006, *Hebrews: A Commentary*, The New Testament Library, Louisville, KY: Westminster John Knox Press.

Jones, Sarah, 2011, *Call Me Evil, Let Me Go: A Mother's Struggle to Save Her Children from a Brutal Religious Cult*, London: Harper Element.

Keenan, Marie, 2012, *Child Sexual Abuse and the Catholic Church: Gender, Power, and Organizational Culture*, New York: Oxford University Press.

Keener, Craig, 1999, *A Commentary on the Gospel of Matthew*, Grand Rapids, MI: Eerdmans.

Keener, Craig, 2003, *The Gospel of John: A Commentary*, Peabody, MA: Hendrickson.

Kvarfordt, Connie L., 'Spiritual Abuse and Neglect of Youth: Reconceptualizing what is known through an investigation of practitioners' experiences', *Journal of Religion and Spirituality in Social Work: Social Thought*, 29 2 (2010), pp.143–64.

Lamb, Amanda, and Timothy Briden, 2020, 'A Report upon the Causes, Conduct and Outcome of Proceedings under the Clergy Discipline Measure 2003 against The Reverend Timothy Davis, formerly Vicar of Christ Church Abingdon', *Diocese of Oxford*, https://oxford.anglican.org/revd-timothy-davis.php, accessed 18.06.2025.

Lane, William L., 1974, *The Gospel of Mark*, The New International Commentary on the New Testament, Grand Rapids, MI: Eerdmans.

Le Donne, Anthony, and Larry Behrendt, 2017, *Sacred Dissonance: The Blessing of Difference in Jewish–Christian Dialogue*, Peabody, MA: Hendrickson Publishers.

Leach, Jane, and Michael Paterson, 2015, *Pastoral Supervision: A Handbook*, 2nd edn, London: SCM Press.

Lee, Mason, 'Prophets and Sour Grapes: Wrestling with theological traditions in homiletical theology', *Theology Today*, 78 (2021), pp. 43–55.

Let There Be Light, 2024, https://www.lettherebelight.life, accessed 20.02.2025.

Levine, Amy-Jill, 2006, *The Misunderstood Jew: The Church and the Scandal of the Jewish Jesus*, New York: HarperOne.

Levine, Amy-Jill, and Marc Zvi Brettler, 2020, *The Bible With and Without Jesus: How Jews and Christians Read the Same Stories Differently*, New York: Harper One.

Longenecker, B. W., 1998, *The Triumph of Abraham's God: The Transformation of Identity in Galatians*, Edinburgh: T&T Clark.

Longman III, Tremper, 1999, *Daniel*, The NIV Application Commentary, Grand Rapids, MI: Zondervan.

BIBLIOGRAPHY

Lord, Janet, 2019, 'The Power of Purple', in Janet Fife and Gilo (eds), *Letters to a Broken Church*, London: Ekklesia, pp. 97–100.

Makin, Keith, 2024, *Independent Learning Lessons Review: John Smyth QC, The Church of England*, 18 October 2024, https://www.churchofengland.org/sites/default/files/2024-11/independent-learning-lessons-review-john-smyth-qc-november-2024.pdf, accessed 20.02.2025.

Maqbool, Aleem, 2024, 'Preacher Abused His Power as "Spiritual Celebrity"', *BBC News*, 1 October 2024, https://www.bbc.co.uk/news/articles/crl808nxjw5o, accessed 20.02.2025.

Maqbool, Aleem, and Steve Swann, 2024, 'Priest Thought to Pose Risk to Children is Paid Off', *BBC News*, 13 August 2024, https://www.bbc.co.uk/news/articles/cv2gj77pvwwo, accessed 20.02.2025.

Martin, Ralph P., 1986, *2 Corinthians*, Word Biblical Commentary 40, Nashville, TN: Thomas Nelson.

Methodist Church, 2016, *Learning for Trainers Delivering 'Creating Safer Spaces' Modules: The Report on the Past Cases Review – Ten Themes*, https://media.methodist.org.uk/media/documents/learning-for-trainers-pcr_IcoLtuG.pdf, accessed 19.06.2025; see also 'PCR Ten Themes and Report', https://www.methodist.org.uk/safeguarding/courage-cost-and-hope-past-cases-review/pcr-ten-themes-and-report/, accessed 20.02.2025.

Methodist Church, 2022, 'Safeguarding Policies, Procedures and Guidance', https://www.methodist.org.uk/safeguarding/policies-procedure-and-information/policies-and-guidance, accessed 20.02.2025.

Michaels, J. Ramsey, 2010, *The Gospel of John*, The New International Commentary on the New Testament, Grand Rapids, MI: Eerdmans.

Mitchell, David F., 'Ezekiel's Presentation of Divine Sovereignty and Human Responsibility', *The Reformed Theological Review*, 76 2 (2017), pp. 73–100.

Morse, Janet M., 2021, *Developing Grounded Theory: The Second Generation Revisited*, 2nd edn, London: Routledge.

Mullen, Wade, 2020, *Something's Not Right: Decoding the Hidden Tactics of Abuse and Freeing Yourself from Its Power*, Carol Stream, IL: Tyndale Momentum.

Murphy, James, 'Beyond "Religion" and "Spirituality": Extending a "meaning systems" approach to explore lived religion', *Archive for the Psychology of Religion*, 39 (2017), pp. 1–26.

Nanos, M. D., 2022, *The Irony of Galatians: Paul's Letter in First-Century Context*, Minneapolis, MN: Fortress Press.

Nye, Catrin, Natalie Truswell and Jamie Bartlett, 2023, 'A Very British Cult: Inside Lighthouse, the life coaching cult that takes over lives', *BBC News*, 5 April 2023, https://www.bbc.co.uk/news/uk-65175712, accessed 20.02.2025.

Oakley, Lisa, 2009, 'The Experience of Spiritual Abuse within the Christian Faith in the UK', PhD dissertation, Manchester Metropolitan University.

Oakley, Lisa, and Justin Humphreys, 2019, *Escaping the Maze of Spiritual Abuse: Creating Healthy Christian Cultures*, London: SPCK.

Oakley, Lisa, and Kathryn Kinmond, 2013, *Breaking the Silence on Spiritual Abuse*, Basingstoke: Palgrave MacMillan.

Oakley, Lisa, and Kathryn Kinmond, 'Developing Safeguarding Policy and Practice for Spiritual Abuse', *The Journal of Adult Protection*, 16 2 (2014), pp. 87–95.

Oakley, Lisa, Kathryn Kinmond and Justin Humphreys, 'Spiritual Abuse in Christian Faith Settings: Definition, policy and practice guidance', *The Journal of Adult Protection*, 20 3/4 (2018), pp. 144–54.

Oakley, Lisa, Kathryn Kinmond, Justin Humphreys and Mor Dioum, 'Safeguarding Children Who Are Exposed to Abuse Linked to Faith or Belief', *Child Abuse Review*, 28 (2019), pp. 27–38.

O'Callaghan, Denis, 'Sexual Abuse and Spiritual Abuse', *The Furrow*, 51 12 (2000), pp. 693–94.

Overman, J. Andrew, 1990, *Matthew's Gospel and Formative Judaism: The Social World of the Matthean Community*, Minneapolis, MN: Fortress Press.

Overman, J. Andrew, 1996, *Church and Community in Crisis: The Gospel According to Matthew*, Valley Forge, PA: Trinity Press International.

Palmer, Parker J., 1998, *The Courage to Teach: Exploring the Inner Landscape of a Teacher's Life*, San Francisco, CA: Jossey-Bass Publishers.

Paterson, Michael, 2020, *Between a Rock and a Hard Place: Pastoral Supervision Revisited and Revisioned*, Institute of Pastoral Supervision and Reflective Practice.

Pettigrew, Thomas, and Linda Tropp, 'A Meta-Analytic Test of Intergroup Contact Theory', *Journal of Personality and Social Psychology*, 90 (2006), pp. 751–83.

Poirier, John C., 'Another Look at the "Man Born Blind" in John 9', *Journal of Religion, Disability and Health*, 14 (2010), pp. 60–5.

Ranson, David, 'The Climate of Sexual Abuse', *The Furrow*, 53 7/8 (2002), pp. 387–97.

Redman, Matt, 2024, *Let there Be Light* [video], YouTube, 9 April 2024, https://www.youtube.com/watch?v=YVZkgdt32u8, accessed 20.02.2025.

Resane, K. Thomas, 'Leadership for the Church: The shepherd model', *HTS Theological Studies*, 70 (2014), pp. 1–6.

Robertson, O. Palmer, 1990, *The Books of Nahum, Habakkuk, and Zephaniah*, The New International Commentary on the Old Testament, Grand Rapids, MI: Eerdmans.

Schlehofer, Michele M., Allen M. Omoto and Janice R. Adelman, 'How Do "Religion" and "Spirituality" Differ? Lay definitions among older adults', *Journal for the Scientific Study of Religion*, 47 3 (2008), pp. 411–25.

Scolding, Fiona, and Ben Fullbrook, 2024, 'Independent Review into Soul Survivor', 26 September 2024, https://static1.squarespace.com/

static/547c7dfde4b028a1612a4736/t/67640bf60e696221e51d3 08d/1734609912112/Soul+Survivor+Review+-+Updated+Final+Report+181224+PDF.pdf, accessed 20.02.2025.

Scolding, Fiona, Alasdair Henderson and Ben Fullbrook, 2025, 'Independent Review into New Wine', *New Wine*, 12 February 2025, https://www.new-wine.org/app/uploads/2025/02/Independent-Review-into-New-Wine-1.pdf, accessed 20.02.2025.

Segura-April, Desiree, 2016, 'Appropriate Child Participation and the Risks of Spiritual Abuse', *Transformation*, 33 3 (2016), pp. 171–84.

Sikh Women's Aid, n.d., https://www.sikhwomensaid.org.uk, accessed 20.02.2025.

Smith, Caroline E., Duane F. Reinert, Maryanne Horne, Joanne M. Greer and Robert Wicks, 'Childhood Abuse and Spiritual Development among Women Religious', *Journal of Religion and Health*, 34 2 (1995), pp. 127–33.

Smith, Ralph L., 1984, *Micah–Malachi*, Word Biblical Commentary 32, Nashville, TN: Thomas Nelson.

Social Research Association, 2021, 'Research Ethics Guidance', https://the-sra.org.uk/common/Uploaded%20files/Resources/SRA%20Research%20Ethics%20guidance%202021.pdf, accessed 20.02.2025.

Starr, Keshet, 'Scars of the Soul: Get refusal and spiritual abuse in Orthodox Jewish communities', *Nashim: A Journal of Jewish Women's Studies and Gender Issues*, 31 (2017), pp. 37–60.

Steyn, Gert, 'Trajectories of Scripture Transmission: The case of Amos 5.25–27 in Acts 7.42–43', *HTS Theological Studies*, 69 (2013), pp. 1–9.

Stirling, Mark, 2023, 'Introduction: Why another book on power and why now?', in Mark Stirling and Mark Meynell (eds), *Not So with You: Power and Leadership in the Church*, Eugene, OR: Wipf and Stock, pp. xiii–xv.

Stone, Alyson M., 'Thou Shalt Not: Treating religious trauma and spiritual harm with combined therapy', *Eastern Group Psychotherapy Society*, 37 4 (2013), pp. 323–37.

Strine, C. A., 'The Role of Repentance in the Book of Ezekiel: A second chance for a second generation', *The Journal of Theological Studies*, 63 2 (2012), pp. 467–91.

thirtyone:eight, 2021, 'Independent Lessons Learned Review (incorporating an Audit of Safeguarding Arrangements) Concerning Jonathan Fletcher and Emmanuel Church Wimbledon', 23 March 2021, https://thirtyoneeight.org/media/gk1dnt14/independent-lessons-learned-review-report_march-2021.pdf, accessed 20.2.2025.

Thomaskutty, Johnson, 'The Irony of Ability and Disability in John 9.1–41', *HTS Theological Studies*, 78 4 (2022), pp. 1–7.

Ward, David J., 'The Lived Experience of Spiritual Abuse', *Mental Health, Religion & Culture*, 14 9 (2011), pp. 899–915.

Ward, Frances, 2005, *Lifelong Learning: Theological Education and Supervision*, London: SCM Press.

Ward, Frances, 2019, *Full of Character: A Christian Approach to Education for the Digital Age*, London: Jessica Kingsley Publishing.

Weinstein, Yana, and Megan Sumeracki, with Oliver Caviglioli, 2019, *Understanding How We Learn: A Visual Guide*, Abingdon: Routledge.

Westbrook, Lynn, "I'm Not a Social Worker": An information service model for working with patrons in crisis', *The Library Quarterly: Information, Community, Policy*, 85 (2015), pp. 6–25.

White, Amy, 2021, *Towards a Theological Definition of Spiritual Abuse: Ezekiel 34 and the Use of Pastoral Power*, Cambridge: Grove Books.

Wilson, Tom, 2020, *Jesus and the Ioudaioi: Reading John's Gospel with Jewish People in Mind*, Newcastle upon Tyne: Cambridge Scholars.

Wilson, Tom, 2022, *His Blood Be Upon Us: Completion and Condemnation in Matthew's Gospel*, Bradford: Ethics International Press.

Witherington III, Ben, 1998, *Grace in Galatia: A Commentary on St Paul's Letter to the Galatians*, Edinburgh: T&T Clark.

Witherington III, Ben, 2011, *Paul's Letter to the Philippians: A Socio-Rhetorical Commentary*, Grand Rapids, MI: Eerdmans.

www.ingramcontent.com/pod-product-compliance
Lightning Source LLC
Chambersburg PA
CBHW020531080526
44583CB00013B/822